War No More?

War No More?

Options in Nuclear Ethics

Edited and Introduced by
James W. Walters

Fortress Press   Minneapolis

War No More?
Options in Nuclear Ethics

Biblical quotations, unless otherwise noted, are from the Revised Standard Version of the Bible, copyright 1946, 1952, © 1971, 1973 by the Division of Christian Education of the National Council of the Churches of Christ in the U.S.A., and are used by permission.

Cover design: Carol Evans-Smith
Internal design: Peregrine Publications

Library of Congress Cataloging-in-Publication Data

War no more? : options in nuclear ethics / edited and introduced by
   James W. Walters.
      p.   cm.
   Bibliography: p.
   ISBN 0-8006-2333-9
   1. Nuclear warfare—Religious aspects—Christianity. 2. Nuclear
warfare—Moral and ethical aspects.   I. Walters, James W. (James
Williams), 1945-
BR115.A85W36   1989
261.8'732—dc20   89-11995
                                                                          CIP

Printed in the United States of America   1-2333

Contents

Preface

CHRISTIANS CONFESS that the life and teaching of Jesus have a significant impact on their view of the world and how life ought to be lived—and defended. Yet public Christian figures like Jerry Falwell and William Sloane Coffin, Jr., are miles apart on such basic, fundamental questions as the morality and purpose of national defense and nuclear arms. Indeed, Christian diversity on nuclear arms may rival or mirror the pluralistic range of opinion in American society generally on this most monumental question of our time.

Is there an authentic Christian stance toward national policy on the development, possession, and use of nuclear arms? What are the main relevant strands of Christian Scriptures, tradition, and life that thoughtful Christian reflection must consider?

In the last decade serious exchange among scholars, ethicists, church bodies, and peace groups has produced no consensus. Yet it has stirred the minds and consciences of American Christians and crystallized the fundamental Christian options on these questions. The contributors to this volume were chosen precisely because of their diverse views of Christianity's contribution to the nuclear arms discussion. They present, in a succinct and persuasive manner, three distinct options contending in the arena of contemporary Christian thought on nuclear arms. They invite the reader to consider the arguments and their truth claims.

The idea of a brief volume for use by individuals, adult discussion groups, clergy, and undergraduates on comparative Christian thought on nuclear arms emerged from a conference held at Loma Linda University in 1986. Although only a single chapter of this book—the one by William Spohn—was presented there, the conference prefigured this volume in its theme and principal speakers. Organizations that sponsored the originating conference and thus made this volume possible are Loma Linda University's Ethics Center, Graduate School, and Faculty Senate; Interfaith Center to Reverse the Arms Race, Pasadena; Program in Religious Studies, University of California, Riverside; Loma Linda University Church; and Physicians for Social Responsibility, Riverside/San Bernardino chapter.

My special thanks are extended to Raymond Cottrell, Fritz Guy, David Larson, Gwen Utt, and Louis Venden for the different and invaluable contributions of each in making this volume a reality. The authors merit my deepest gratitude for their diligent efforts in producing the fine essays that promise to make this modest volume of comparative Christian thought useful in numerous settings.

James W. Walters
Claremont, California

Contributors

JOHN HOWARD YODER, a noted pacifist theologian, has served as seminary president, university faculty senate chair, Society of Christian Ethics president, and frequent adviser to the World Council of Churches. A voluminous writer, Yoder has published scores of scholarly articles and a dozen books, the most widely known being *The Politics of Jesus* (Wm. B. Eerdmans, 1972). From his base as a professor of historical theology at Notre Dame University, Mennonite Yoder exercises international leadership in theology and ethics.

WILLIAM C. SPOHN, S.J., is associate professor of Christian ethics at the Jesuit School of Theology, Berkeley. Spohn's latest book is *What Are They Saying about Scripture?* (Paulist Press, 1986). Spohn has a special interest in the relationship of Christian faith to the nuclear arms threat.

PAUL SEABURY has served as professor of political science at the University of California, Berkeley, since 1953. He was a member of President Ronald Reagan's Foreign Intelligence Advisory Board, 1982-85. Seabury serves on the executive committee of Freedom House, New York City. Of the 11 books Seabury has written or edited, *The Red Orchestra* (Hoover Institute Press, 1986) is his most recent. He has published numerous scholarly articles and articles in such journals of opinion as *The New Republic, Harpers,* and *Commentary.*

JOHN C. BENNETT, after a long, distinguished career as theologian, ecumenist, and educator, is retired in Claremont, California. His first book was *Social Salvation* (Scribners, 1935) and his latest, coauthored with Harvey Seifert, is *U.S. Foreign Policy and Christian Ethics* (Westminster, 1977). Bennett has received honorary degrees from Harvard, Yale, Princeton, and 18 other institutions of higher learning. In addition to various leadership roles in church and community, Bennett served as cochairman of the Geneva Conference on Church and Society, 1966. Bennett served as professor of Christian ethics at Union Theological Seminary from 1943 to 1970 and as its president from 1963 to 1970.

GEORGE WEIGEL, a Roman Catholic theologian, is president of the Ethics and Public Policy Center, Washington, D.C., and editor of *American Purpose.* His book, *Tranquillitas Ordinis: The Present Failure and Future Promise of American Catholic Thought on War and Peace,* was published in 1987 by the Oxford University Press. From 1977 to 1984, Weigel was Scholar-in-Residence at the World without War Council, Seattle. His latest book is *Catholicism and the Renewal of American Democracy,* published in 1989 by Paulist Press.

JAMES W. WALTERS, is an associate professor of Christian ethics at Loma Linda University. He is the author and editor of three books and numerous essays. His primary professional responsibilities are in the area of biomedical ethics, and he is currently working on a book that develops criteria for determining the value of marginal human life.

Introduction

DESPITE THE enormous stakes involved and the huge national resources expended, the entire U.S. nuclear defense posture rests on some fragile—and surprisingly fluid—assumptions.

In fact, Americans may be forgiven some confusion about the best course for their nuclear policy to take. In the last decade, the citizenry has been bombarded by a full range of nuclear policy options—nuclear freeze, negotiated limits, negotiated reductions in weaponry, no first use, strategic defense initiative (SDI), build up and build down, and even limited nuclear war.

What are the assumptions about ourselves and our responsibility that govern our thinking about nuclear arms? This volume is intended to help its readers clarify their own stance. It focuses not on defining our national interests nor divining the intentions of our adversaries nor gauging our strategic situation but on the fundamental clash of systems of moral thinking presented by the nuclear question. It asks whether Christian commitment illumines the momentous issue of modern war and peace.

Jesus, of course, did not consider nuclear weapons nor forge national policy. But he did face personal and communal questions on the use of violence, and he defined a position in word and deed. Jesus' teaching and example are at least a datum for contemporary thinking. Admittedly, Jesus' historical situation might not be a paradigm here, but more important is the gestalt regarding peace and violence that he projected. And a gestalt— a basic, intuitive sense—is often the prerational base that reason and argument merely fill out.

What view of war can defensibly be put forward as fundamentally Christian? What is so important in life that a Christian is justified in spilling blood—others' and one's own? Answers vary according to the weight given to the earliest interpreters of Jesus (his first disciples) or to a variety of later followers (bishops and theologians). In any case, invoking the name of Christ is not the last word in the discussion. It is but the first step in exploration of presuppositions for Christian thinking on modern warfare. The fundamental question of this volume is: What do Christians have to say about nuclear deterrence and war? Presently in the U.S., three main positions contend for the Christian conscience, and in this book three leading Christian thinkers present the options.

Christian Pacifism. A simple answer is that of doctrinaire pacifism: absolutely nothing justifies the spilling of human blood; it is un-Christian and hence immoral and always wrong. Such a pacifist view takes this message as the prima facie reading of Jesus' life and refuses to countenance any bloodshed—violence begets violence.

Christian pacifism, literally, "Christian peace making," was prominent in the early church. Whether antipathy toward the Roman Empire or faithfulness to a Christian ideal was the primary impetus is debated. Regardless, Roland Bainton's comment is apt: "All of the outstanding writers of the East and West repudiated participation in warfare for Christians."[1] After Constantine's conversion in the fourth century, the church legitimated lay participation in just wars, but forbade clerical participation due to higher demands of perfection. Historically, the

Waldenses and some Anabaptists have been pacifists, as have been many members of the "historic peace churches"—Quakers, Mennonites, and the Brethren. James Childress identifies three major types of contemporary pacifism: (1) Nuclear pacifism holds that although conditions might exist that excuse or even compel conventional warfare, nuclear war is totally unjustifiable. (2) Pragmatic pacifism, usually presupposing an optimistic view of human nature, contends that pacifism is a practical strategy for achieving a net balance of good over evil. (3) Deontological pacifism sees war as a violation of the commandment against killing, the New Testament norm of neighbor-love, and discipleship in the suffering church community.[2] (Deontology is a school of ethical decision making that focuses on present duty, even though untoward consequences might occur.)

John Howard Yoder, a leading proponent of Christian pacifism, begins the discussion by advocating a mixed deontological-pragmatic pacifism. Rather than calling for an absolute renunciation of force, Yoder's "Nuclear Arms in Christian Pacifist Perspective" supports creative, nonviolent resistance and criticizes the dehumanizing and self-serving nature of all war.

Just War. The second camp is that of the just warriors. They hold that certain forms of war may be justified if the cause is right. For example, many if not most American Christians would hold that a free, democratic society is worth dying—and killing—for. But how many combatants and innocent lives justifiably can be sacrificed for what is held to be a just cause? In light of the reality that no human government is ideal, drawing lines is necessary. Few Christians contend that World War II was immoral even though 50 million lives were lost. Thus the Western—if not American—way of life is worth a conventional war in the minds of most Christian and secular citizens. But what about a nuclear war? A "minor" intercontinental nuclear war might cost five or six times the World War II toll, and a major conflagration many times that—both involving hundreds of millions of innocent citizens.

The just-war tradition is the legacy of Christian thinkers since Augustine who have set forth minimal moral conditions for Christian participation in war. The presupposition is that conditions might indeed exist that legitimate a Christian's use, albeit a reluctant use, of violence. In personal matters, an innocent neighbor under attack by an assailant should be aided in the name of charity, reasoned Augustine. To protect the Roman Empire from invading Germanic peoples, Christian soldiers fought for the life of their supposedly innocent kingdom. Historically, the conditions for justifiable war were rightful authority, just cause, and proper means. Today, criteria such as proportionality of destruction, discrimination in targeting, and probability of success are cited. Whether a nuclear war could meet modern just-war criteria is widely suspect. Because many just-war theorists are skeptical, pacifism—at least the nuclear variety—is receiving considerable attention.

Just-war reasoning is a compromise between political realism and moral ideals. "The just war norms arise from a consideration of how the basic values of life, freedom, justice, etc., are related to each other in the light of our historical experience and our practical understanding of the functioning of the political order. They are norms of political morality, and as such they are a synthesis of both political and moral commitment," writes David Hollenbach.[3]

William Spohn, a Jesuit colleague of Hollenbach, analyzes the Catholic bishops' pastoral letter on nuclear arms in his "Nuclear Deterrence under Strict Moral Conditions." In appreciation of the traditional Catholic belief that some acts are intrinsically evil and hence never to be done, he criticizes the pastoral letter for its conditional acceptance of nuclear deterrence: "I do not see how any form of deterrence can be both credible and moral."

Just Nuclear Defense. The third option examined in this volume is the argument that a nuclear war itself may need to be fought to protect precious political or religious values. A foremost proponent of such reasoning is Michael Novak, who has maintained that Western political institutions, such as democracy, freedom of the press, and private property, lie so close to the spiritual core of Western civilization as to justify competing in an arms race or even fighting a nuclear war to preserve them.[4] Although most Christian ethicists reject the contention that nuclear war can be justified on any basis, some Christian thinkers believe that a nuclear war could meet the moral criteria for a just war. Such a war must be (1) limited—the use of tactical nuclear weapons on the battlefield, or one-at-a-time strategic strikes; (2) counterforce-oriented, as opposed to counterpopulation; and (3) graduated, in that only sufficient nuclear force is used as needed to deter further enemy aggression. The argument is furthered by pointing to the technological advances that allow for precise targeting and that have reduced the yield and collateral radiation effects of nuclear warheads. Just nuclear defense advocates see themselves combining a hardheaded realism about the permanence of nuclear weapons with traditional religious justification of war within moral constraints.

Paul Seabury, in contrast to Spohn, writes that the Christian just-war tradition leads not to an abandonment of nuclear deterrence but rather to its strengthening. In his essay, "The Just-War Legacy in the Nuclear Age," Seabury views failure to use whatever means available to prevent the overthrow of basic American freedoms and liberties as the zenith of immorality. After laying out his own position, the author severely criticizes the positions of both Yoder and Spohn.

The book concludes with commentaries on the essays and dialog written by two distinguished scholars writing from opposite points of view. John Coleman Bennett is a distinguished liberal Protestant theologian who has thought and written about Christianity and war for more than 50 years. George Weigel, director of the Ethics and Public Policy Center, a politically conservative think tank in Washington, D.C., is a leading neo-conservative student of nuclear war who has questioned whether the heritage of just-war theory has been abused by those who exclude nuclear war from its aegis.[5]

Nuclear Arms in Christian Pacifist Perspective

John Howard Yoder

An Array of Possible Answers

A strictly logical analysis demonstrates five possible ways to respond to the moral challenge of war. Political philosopher Michael Walzer refers to one possibility as "insanity," "frenzy," "intoxication," and "hysteria"—the abandonment, willing and witting or not, of moral control.[1] It appears paradoxical to refer to the abandonment of restraint as one moral option. Yet there are structured ways to express this view, which one finds in the arts, in education and propaganda, in psychology. Not to acknowledge its presence would be to fail to relate moral thought to the realities of the case. Serious emotional claims have been made in America recently for macho self-affirmation as a cure for "the Vietnam syndrome."

Another possibility, affirming the moral ultimacy of national interest, Walzer calls "realism."[2] As early as the general response to Machiavelli and Grotius's response to the cynic Carneades, many have seen this view as cynical or as amoral. That may be the case, but it can also be accountable. For those who gave modern currency and credibility to the term *realism,* especially Hans Morgenthau and Reinhold Niebuhr, it was eminently an expression of moral responsibility.

Yet another view is the "holy war," in which a particular cause, usually one's own, is said to be divinely commanded. Classically we associate this attitude with Moses and Joshua, Mohammed, St. Bernard, and the Ayatollah Khomeini. But the "god" in whose name some claim an absolute moral mandate may also be the blood and soil of Nazism or the historical necessity of some Marxists. What defines this approach formally is the way in which the moral authorization for war is perceived transcendentally, independently of any need to measure the empirical political acts or to recognize the rights of adversaries.

A fourth possibility is the "justifiable war," according to which one can calculate, on the basis of several criteria, testing the cause, the means, the authority . . .[3] when a given military option, . . . though evil, is considered less evil than the threat it opposes.

"Pacifism," the fifth possibility, rejects all of the above on basic moral grounds. Some use the term *pacifism* more loosely, speaking, for example, of nuclear pacifism to describe applying just-war criteria to nuclear weapons or even to describe applying self-centered "realism" to a situation in which weapons have become uncontrollable.

The pacifist option may be taken on various grounds, religious or philosophical. In a Christian context pacifism has found expression in varied moral phraseology:[4]

The simple prohibition of the shedding of blood

Avoidance of the idolatry that validated and sanctified the Roman military establishment[5]

Obedience to the law of Christ, who radicalizes the prohibition of killing into the imperative of love for the enemy[6]

Conformity to the example of Jesus Christ, the suffering servant and revealer of the divine will[7]

Knowing a power that does away with all war[8]

Honoring "that of God in everyone"[9]

Cultivating the virtue of meekness, which resigns a person to lack of control of the world.[10]

My task here is not to decide the relative validity of these forms of expression or their interrelationship, nor yet to synthesize them (or their more modern counterparts). Instead, from a stance within the stream of Christian community and experience that they represent, it is my purpose to restate, in classical Christian language, the grounds for a continuing moral rejection of war and to note the way in which pacifism's rejection of war differs from the other standard models.[11]

He Is Our Peace

First but not foremost, Jesus is presented—with special clarity in Matthew's Gospel—as teacher of the fulfillment of the law. There, love for one's enemy stands, on both literary and substantive grounds, as the prime specimen of the newness of the age. Jesus is the herald of that new age before he is the teacher of the new Torah. Tolstoy made the case on literary grounds: the center of the Gospel according to Matthew is the Sermon on the Mount. The center of the Sermon on the Mount is the six antitheses in chapter 5, and the center of the antitheses is "Resist not the evil one."

As teacher of the new Torah, Jesus is herald of the new age. The difference between the old age and the new is that the former ethic reserved love for one's near neighbor or compatriot. Now the privileged object of love is the distant neighbor, the enemy. This change is not an arbitrary fluctuation in an erratically changing system of rules, but a clarification or "fulfillment" of the law's initial purpose. Even more basic, it is a revelation of God's own nature.[12]

In addition to being herald and rabbi, or teacher, Jesus came as liberator. That is the root meaning, both historical and etymological, of the name Jesus. It is the historically developed meaning of the name Anointed *(mashiach, christos)*. It was the point at issue in the public ministry of Jesus as presented in the Gospel record, whose temptation accounts center on whether Jesus should use violence in the interest of political righteousness.

Beyond the above, Jesus is acknowledged as Lord, *kyrios,* which in the first century made him leader not only of the church—that is, of those who confessed his name—but also of persons and human authorities who did not. Later theologies used the word *providence* for the same notion. This means that the course of history is ultimately in his hands despite the rebelliousness of the persons and powers who *seem* to be in charge. Believers need neither despair nor sell out when it *seems* that the only way to defend God's cause is to abandon God's way.

Jesus is further confessed as Word, *logos,* the one in whose life and work God's nature and will are made tangible in human affairs. This undercuts our usual idea that there may be other "words" or ways by which to know God's will than what Jesus taught and exemplified. The firmest form of the affirmation that there are other, contradictory norms to weigh against Jesus is probably the high Reformed conception of the orders of Creation. The clearest contemporary rejection of such a competitive claim is the confession of Barmen: "Jesus Christ . . . is the one Word of God. We repudiate the false teaching that the Church can and must recognize yet other happenings and powers, images and truths as divine revelation alongside this one Word. . . ."[13]

Jesus rose and ascended to the right hand of the Father, whence he shall come to judge the world. Despite appearances, the providential guidance of events and their ultimate denouement is the work not of autonomous mechanisms or anonymous powers, but of the same will and power that those who knew him personally "saw" and "touched" (1 John 1:1)—the man Jesus. It is thus illegitimate to conceive of human events merely as the result of human strategy, intrigue, and manipulation, as if it were an autonomous, self-contained causal system.

Jesus promised to send the Spirit to lead his followers into all truth. The bridge between Jesus' teaching in the long ago and our present obedience is not a matter of intellectual deduction or extrapolation. It is not a matter of guesswork or of devising a chain of historical cause-and-effect relationships, but of the continuing presence of the same divine power and will through the Spirit.

The Changing Face of the Moral Issue

What seems to many to have changed in recent years is the coincidence of practical conclusions dictated by various systems on different grounds. Just-war axioms are operating when Roman Catholic bishops of the United States[14] or the World Council of Churches[15] apply the criteria of discrimination, proportion, and especially noncombatant immunity as a basis on which to condemn the present arms race.[16] This is fundamental progress. It makes the just-war tradition potentially credible. It is *not*, however, to say that the just-war approach is being applied with growing sincerity and accountability across the board. The other criteria of the traditional just-war doctrine (cause, authority, intention, probability of success, and respect for international law) are receiving far less rigorous attention.

A third party, who might be called "realists," has recently joined the practical coalition between traditional pacifism and nuclear pacifism. The prospect of nuclear fallout, retaliation, and nuclear winter are beginning to convince these realists that the arms race is counterproductive even apart from moral considerations.

Thus the *face* of the question of war is changing, not because any one of the three basic positions—pacifism, just war, or realism—has been abandoned or fundamentally changed, but because political and technological changes have led partisans of the three positions to parallel tactics. On the level of public awareness this development is of major importance and may offer an opportunity for dialog and still further change, though in terms of ethics it is superficial.

Our task here is to look beyond the present tactical coalition against nuclear destruction, to identify the significant abiding differences in basic ethical method. The 1983 United States Bishops' pastoral letter—*The Challenge of Peace: God's Promise and Our Response*—will suffice as a basis for identifying these differences, inasmuch as it is more fully reasoned than any other recent statement.[17]

First, the bishops' letter holds that one can stockpile nuclear weapons as a deterrent while excluding their use, pending progress in disarmament. This notion is politically and psychologically unrealistic.[18]

22

Second, the letter avers that the just-war theory and pacifism are the only two ways in which Christians have thought about the morality of war. This is true only of theologians and saints. Wars that most bishops have blessed and most Christians have died in for a millennium and a half have been wars of national interest subject to no moral restraint, and "holy" wars for which transcendental authority was claimed. The letter's failure to be frank about failures of the past is part of its failure to come to grips with the present.

A third difference in ethical method can be seen in the bishops' list of just-war criteria *ad bellum* (grounds for going to war). It is relatively correct, but their letter does nothing to apply them. It appears to assume that the criteria of cause, authority, and last resort are never likely to be problematic in American experience. It attends only to the *in bello* (means of waging war) criteria of discrimination, proportion, and innocent immunity. It ignores the question of respect for international law, customs, and treaties. In short, it considers only a few of the classical criteria rather than all or most of the multidimensional aspects of the just-war tradition.

Fourth, like most recent statements, *The Challenge of Peace* fails to specify what should take place in a given situation when the just-war restraints are clearly not being respected. Logically, there would be selective disobedience on the part of participants, or a cessation of hostilities on the part of the governments involved. *The Challenge of Peace* ignores the latter possibility and merely suggests the former.

Fifth, by beginning with the damage a massive exchange would cause, the bishops' argument demonstrates the certain inadmissibility of all-out nuclear war, but it leaves uncertain the locus of the actual threshold of inadmissibility further down the scale, and thereby suggests willingness to haggle about less destructive levels.

23

Recognition of these shortcomings of *The Challenge of Peace* is not to refute the just-war tradition but to respect it. It is not to make light of the letter but to note how far it has come along a lengthy path. The just-war tradition is a many-dimensioned discipline, all of whose facets require honest, forthright consideration.

The Qualities of a Credible Just-War Thesis

To be credible, the claim that war as the lesser of two evils is morally permissible would require the following elements: (1) Citizens, government officials, and military officials fully instructed with respect to criteria by which to determine whether or not war would be justified; (2) An independent source of information to ascertain the factual basis on which to determine whether war would meet the restraints of cause, authority, last resort, and probability of success; (3) A consensus of the various agencies of moral insight (churches, universities, think tanks, media) so that the limits of obedience may be determined on grounds that are not aritrary: (4) An unambiguous, objective definition of "last resort"; (5) Clarity as to whether an infraction in the conduct of a just war disqualifies it as just; and (6) Accountable criteria for measuring the notion of "proportion" between one evil and another.

The more accurately just-war advocates apply these criteria the closer they will come to a pacifism based on moral principles, and the more effective their common front will be against the real adversaries—national interest, holy war, and jingoistic militarism.

The Clash of Moral Systems

To many, the essential point at issue in the three alternatives being considered appears at first to be between consequential reasoning, which justifies war on the grounds of preventing a greater evil; and deontological rigidity, which altogether disregards historical reality in preference for what it considers moral purity. A prima facie analysis suggests a basic clash between ethical styles. Both the realist model and the justifiable war model are fundamentally consequential in their reasoning. They assume (1) that certain objectives are self-evidently valid; (2) that the cause-and-effect relationship involved is transparently evident, so that a choice between alternative courses of action is directly equivalent to a choice between two ultimate outcomes; and (3) that we are able to impose our preference upon the course of events. These assumptions are taken to be self-evident rather than tested in the crucible of reality.

As a matter of fact, there are few circumstances under which these assumptions would stand up under critical examination. Even were they to be empirically appropriate—that is, if we could be certain that a particular course of action would produce the desired result, if we had all the power necessary to achieve it, and if we knew for sure which outcome would prove to be most useful—this pragmatic concept of a causally closed world is refuted by the biblical concept of Christ's lordship.

Accordingly, the first level of dialog should address the ways in which the above assumptions fail to obtain.[19] In most instances we do not have access to enough facts, or an adequate grasp of cause-and-effect relationships, or enough power to make reliable moral decisions on the basis of the preferred outcome of a resort to violence in contrast with what we would lose without it.

25

John Howard Yoder

However, this is not to grant that justified-war reasoning is authentically pragmatic. It is certainly less so than prima facie naiveté assumes. Neither does pacifism renounce consequential analysis; we shall return to the prudential side of nonviolence. It is, however, the case that those to whom just-war responses seem most self-evident naively reason in terms of what they consider to be also self-evident pragmatic goals. Renunciation of military action is thought to jeopardize those goals and war is thought sure to obtain them. Thus—on the level of prima facie analysis—it would seem to those who so reason that the pacifist follows a "divine command" postulate.

But that line of reasoning is simplistic. The ideological clash can be better described as a difference regarding the values each position seeks to defend—that is, the causes each considers just. Values clash: the sacredness of life versus the defense of a preferred political system, the human dignity of the "enemy" versus self-interest, the worldwide community versus the parties directly involved. It is deceptive to claim to characterize real moral debates in terms of abstract ethical analysis (deontology, consequences, character, etc.). Every serious moral commitment involves at least tacitly a set of assumptions in each of those columns. The just-war stance claims at first to be merely hard-nosed about effectiveness, but first it has to be deontological (duty-oriented) about one's own government's claims to legitimacy. The realist claims to eschew transcendent warrants but thereby dodges accountability for the choice as to who has the right to make the definitions of national interest.

Although I have, for the purpose of discussion, taken note of the challenge of consequentialism because it is philosophically important, I do not grant that the other views of the morality of war are consistently pragmatic, or that pacifism is alone deontological. The "realistic" view is utterly and uncritically deontological about the claims of the nation to which it subordinates everyone else's rights. The just-war tradition is deontological with respect to noncombatant immunity and just cause; the "hysterical" perspective is quite unpragmatic. But now our point is that an ethic of principle is quite practical.

The Power of Truth Rediscovered

There was a time when moral thought in the "divine command" mode of just war seemed to center upon a negative understanding of "do not resist the evil one" (Matt. 5:39), with "nonresistance" enshrined as a principled rejection of social involvement. Through the 19th century, some of the language of Tolstoy, and of Ballou and Garrison, could be taken as calling for such an abdication of concern for social impact, although their behavior did not confirm that view.[20] It was Tolstoy's profound moral simplicity that led Gandhi to create a new kind of agency for resistance and social renewal. What Gandhi learned from Tolstoy and others, and what Martin Luther King, Jr. and others learned from Gandhi, was that a firm moral commitment to the human dignity of the adversary makes possible a new kind of social effectiveness.[21] Gandhi said it in terms of soul power *(satyagraha)*. He titled his autobiography, "My Experiments with Truth," because it charted his learning about the power of truth telling. To resist the oppressor nonviolently is not a posture of weakness but of power.

In part, the powerful effect of loving one's enemy is subject to analysis in terms of standard sociological understandings of communication and causation. Social science can explain why truth telling has a tactical advantage against centralized information manipulation, why the noncooperation of the poor can outwait and outsuffer the strength of the rich, how the grass-roots community can build a stronger solidarity than the hier-archies and bureaucracies of the establishment. It is therefore quite possible to transpose or translate the strategies of non-violence—and even the underlying views of personality and society—into nonsectarian terms.[22]

The just-war mode of argument cannot honestly refuse to take account of changing perspectives on alternative modes of power. The criteria of proportion and of last resort must function differently if we realize that there are hitherto untested instru-ments of conflict management, defense, and social change, which use power in the service of valid ends and which run risks but do not make institutional provision for lethal violence.

Yet neither Gandhi nor King would have been satisfied with such a transposition, as if one could without remainder abstract a form of behavior out of the world view in which it first made sense. Both men reached back behind any pragmatic argumentation when they refused (in their terms) to separate ends and means. For them, such a separation opened the pos-sibility that, in extreme cases, violent means might be justified by the claim better to serve some just end. This possibility they refused to consider. It is important that they did not grant that one can put the question that way. Likewise it is important that their refutation did not proceed by way of a promise that they could face all possible tactical challenges and always win without killing. They rather made a philosophical or a theological claim, a statement about the shape of the world: namely, that ends and means are inseparable. Gandhi said this on Hindu grounds, according to which reincarnation and the great chain of being guarantee that *ultimately* means and ends must coincide. King said the same thing in his own combination of black Baptist biblical hope, Boston University personalism, and mainline hu-manism.

One of King's frequent rhetorical resources was the poem by James Russell Lowell:

> Will the cause of evil prosper?
> Yet 'tis truth alone is strong.
> Though her portion be the scaffold,
> And upon the throne be wrong.
> Yet that scaffold sways the future,
> and behind the dim unknown
> Standeth God within the shadow,
> Keeping watch above His own.

That the cross rules the future, that God watches in the shadow, is for King (as for Lowell) not mere poetic hyperbole. It is a carefully considered, historically warranted, religious world view. The unity of ends and means is ultimately a religious world view, one which incorporates rather than rejects pragmatic wisdom. It thereby rejects the pragmatist's question (effectiveness or faithfulness?) rather than the pragmatist's answer (effectiveness).

A more petty form of the effectiveness debate is the question put to the critic of violence: Can one, in all possible circumstances, avoid all possible violence? or Can one avoid all possible crunch or collision situations in which one would have to fall short of absolute obedience? Can there not be situations when there is only the choice between someone's death and someone else's death? Or between someone's death and telling a lie? Of course there can be such cases. There is nothing about a principled morality that requires us to promise that there can be no hard cases.

There are views that promise divine intervention, whereby persons can claim to keep intact a principled ethic with no exceptions. But then what is subject to debate is a particular conception of miracle or providence, not the principled ethic.[23] There are also pragmatists and realists and (especially) crusaders who count on saving divine intervention to guarantee the success of violent causes. What is denied in careful ethics is that the solution to each hard case should be to prefer one's own immediate interest to that of others. What is wrong with the argument in the present setting is, however, simpler: it is that war is not an extreme collision. War is an institution, the result of long-range planning, equipping, training. I could grant a very wide spectrum of exceptions to the prohibition of killing, on the casuistic edges where general obligations clash, without it following at all that war could be justified. I could grant personal self-defense against the very immediate local threat of brutal aggression, as did Gandhi and Merton, without it following, by any stretch of logic, that the institution of war is acceptable.[24] Hard hypothetical or real cases do not constitute an argument, except against a position that would promise seamless pragmatic perfection as a mark of obedience.

Thus nothing about the pacifist commitment needs to evade the challenge of practical reasoning about attainable ends and effective means. It differs from those who justify war, not in being morally absolute (there is hardly a more absolute claim than to assume the authority to terminate other people's lives), but in weighting differently the priority of values for which one's government is the guarantor, the right of one's neighbors to life and dignity, or of the near neighbor (the compatriot) over that of the far neighbor (the enemy).

Change and Constancy

We conclude that escalation of the nuclear stakes makes no *fundamental* difference in the morality of war. From the just-war perspective it does make a difference, as the data entering into the multifactored calculation of presumably justified, less-evil violence change. For the amoral realist as well, the threat of nuclear suicide makes a difference. These changes having taken place, it is all for the good that just-war thinkers and realists should be honest rather than self-deceiving: the practical coalition of the three different streams is welcome.

Once this coalition has been forced upon them at the top of the scale—the level of all-out nuclear war—the fruitfulness of less violent or nonviolent alternatives in other than the most extreme cases becomes apparent as well. On average and in the long run, love and truth cannot lose because they are in harmony with the inherent nature of human existence.

Nuclear Deterrence under Strict Moral Conditions

William C. Spohn, S.J.

To EXAMINE the problem of nuclear deterrence from a Roman Catholic perspective, I discuss the United States Catholic bishops' pastoral letter *The Challenge of Peace: God's Promise and Our Response,* issued in 1983, and subsequent debates on the moral acceptability of nuclear deterrence. The central issue is whether the threat of nuclear retaliation, which lies at the heart of our national deterrence posture, is morally legitimate.

At the outset we need to indicate how moral theology operates in order to appreciate the form of argumentation that lies behind the theological discussion of deterrence. Roman Catholic moral theology is a complex discipline that attempts to integrate moral wisdom from a variety of sources. Second, we will examine the biblical theology of peace presented in the pastoral letter to grasp both its direction and its ambiguity. Third, we will focus on the application of just-war criteria to nuclear deterrence and the problems inherent in our present national strategic posture.

William C. Spohn, S.J.

Moral Theology

Roman Catholics have a long and complex tradition of reflection on moral issues that draws from four sources: Scripture, tradition, philosophical ethics, and relevant empirical data. Each of these sources has an indispensable role in reaching a balanced theological judgment on a particular moral question. These sources are mutually corrective and complementary. Since *The Challenge of Peace* draws on each of these sources, let us briefly indicate the role each plays.

Scripture. The Bible provides the fundamental norm of Christian identity. Although before the Second Vatican Council biblical material was often used merely to ornament arguments that were primarily philosophical, recent moral theology relies more on biblical themes and perspectives. Particular moral norms of Scripture are placed in the context of God's action in history, definitively expressed in the ministry, death, and resurrection of Jesus Christ. Although we cannot turn to Scripture for particular moral norms on nuclear war, it does provide a vision and "urgent direction when we look at today's concrete realities."[1]

Tradition. Moral questions rarely are novel. By considering the major voices of the Christian tradition, we include their insights in our considerations. Scripture itself is the product of inspired traditions. It is the norm for subsequent handing on of the revelation of God. Tradition includes the church councils and great theologians as well as specific church teaching on moral questions. New developments can call into question certain elements of tradition, as when the Second Vatican Council asked the faithful "to undertake an evaluation of war with an entirely new attitude."[2]

Philosophical Ethics. Based on the theological conviction that God's intentions for human flourishing can be discovered in ordinary human experience, moral theology relies on philosophical reflection to determine what constitutes authentic human morality. It has often relied on "natural law" to determine norms and values that are part of our common humanity. Biblical support for this reliance can be found in Paul's position that the Gentiles possess a moral conscience that corroborates the law revealed through Moses (Rom. 2:12-16).[3]

On questions of warfare, the most consistent line of moral argumentation in the West can be traced back to Augustine. The so-called just-war tradition attempts to restrict the recourse to violence within certain moral boundaries, stemming from the basic human moral obligation: Do no harm to another.

Empirical Data. Human experience on a more empirical level also plays a necessary role in moral reflection. Not only the ordinary experience of people, but also the data made available from biology and the social and psychological sciences can alter traditional moral reflection and correct philosophical speculation. For example, revelation, tradition, and philosophical ethics need to assess the testimony of strategic planners and weapons designers against the identity normative for authentic Christian life.[4]

At its best, therefore, moral theology attempts to integrate wisdom from a number of sources in order to determine what the Christian ought to be and do. Because it has confidence that God's intentions for humanity are not only disclosed in Scripture but also are found in ordinary experience, it believes that believers and nonbelievers can enter into discussion on moral matters. *The Challenge of Peace (CP)* addresses the wider public on the nuclear question, not only the consciences of Christians:

> The wider civil community, although it does not share the same vision of faith, is equally bound by certain key moral

principles. For all men and women find in the depth of
their consciences a law written on the human heart by God.
(CP, 17)

A Catholic approach to the nuclear question, therefore,
will attempt to combine a biblical vision with its traditional
reliance on just-war thinking in order to illuminate a human
response to the threat of nuclear annihilation. It hopes that any
reasonable person of good will would find its presentation persuasive, at least where general human values and moral principles are invoked. Although reason does not exhaust what
biblical revelation discloses, on fundamental moral principles
reason is coherent with the stance of faith. In *The Challenge of
Peace* a biblical theology of peace sets the context for applying
just-war principles to the new situation of threatened mutual
destruction by nuclear arms.

A Biblical Theology of Peace

Although the pastoral letter is mostly devoted to just-war
thinking about the nuclear situation, an important first section
discusses the biblical theology of peace. The argument here is
addressed to those who believe in the God who speaks through
the Scriptures. This treatment represents a significant advance
over traditional Catholic discussion on war and peace since it
presents a more historical notion of God. Natural law argumentation customarily depended on an image of God as Creator
of a relatively stable natural order. Scripture augments this approach by presenting God as one who acts in history, intervening
to save and challenge God's people, and finally manifesting the
full divine design for salvation only in Jesus Christ.[5]

The Challenge of Peace grounds the obligation of peace-making in Christology. This foundation means that we cannot derive our options *as Christians* simply from moral philosophy or natural law. We have to go to the source of that faith, in particular to the person and ministry of Christ. Biblical theology can remind us of our true identity, which should set the framework for moral decision. Whatever option individual Catholics may take on the arms race, it must be compatible with three theological foundations: (1) Christ intended to reconcile all people with God and one another; (2) As his disciples, Christians must continue this work of reconciliation through the community, which is Christ's body; (3) The messianic peace of Christ has already begun but is not yet fulfilled—either in the church or in the world at large. Together these three convictions direct Christian peacemaking in the nuclear age, even if they do not dictate a single strategy that would be agreed upon by all.

The logic of discipleship lies behind the call to be peace-makers. Since Christ's mission was primarily one of reconciliation, his followers must become reconcilers in their own time. They will not primarily seek inner tranquility but must take their pursuit of peace into the public arena where they will attempt to bring together hostile groups and nations and establish the structures of justice, which are the foundations of peace. This work of reconciliation becomes more imperative as we read the ominous signs of the times. Living under the cloud of nuclear extinction, we can appreciate that "the moral issue at stake in nuclear war involves the meaning of sin in its most graphic dimensions" *(CP,* 123). The ministry of reconciliation, therefore, must extend to the sociopolitical arena of the superpowers.

Once we see that reconciliation is at the heart of Christology, we have a key principle to interpret biblical passages. Individual texts cannot be quoted out of context in partisan

William C. Spohn, S.J.

fashion. Pacifists may insist that "turning the other cheek" (Matt. 5:39) obliges all Christians literally, while advocates of military force may absolutize the example of Jesus cleansing the temple (Matt. 21:12-17). The pastoral letter rules out any such proof-text use of Scripture because it insists that any text must be read in light of the vocation to peacemaking that flows from the person of Jesus Christ.

The New Testament offers specific guidance on *how* we are to pursue reconciliation. The story of Jesus shows the dispositions of the heart necessary for Christian peacemaking. His insistence on forgiveness reverses the logic of vengeance. The reign of God rests on love, "an active, life-giving, inclusive force" *(CP,* 47). Although it does not use the language of non-violence explicitly, the pastoral letter portrays Jesus as a man committed to nonretaliation. He defended the rights of others but did not insist on his own: "In all his sufferings, as in all of his life and ministry, Jesus refused to defend himself with force or violence" *(CP,* 49). The culminating event of Jesus' mission defines the path of Christian reconciliation. On the cross he abolished the enmity between God and humanity. As raised from the dead, he thus becomes our peace, the one "who has made us both one, and has broken down the dividing wall of hostility" (Eph. 2:14).

The second biblical theme connects contemporary Christians to Jesus through the logic of discipleship. Biblical stories and exhortations mandate certain dispositions or virtues that ought to guide Christians to act as Jesus did. It also counsels Christians not to expect a more favorable reception for their witness of peace than their master received:

> As disciples and children of God, it is our task to seek for ways in which to make the forgiveness, justice and mercy

and love of God visible in a world where violence and enmity are too often the norm. *(CP,* 55)

The bishops extend this logic of discipleship to the whole church. Since Vatican II, Catholics have come to see that the call to holiness and profound Christian witness is not confined to a certain "professional class" of clergy and members of religious orders. All are called to be disciples, and lay people have a special vocation to witness in the sociopolitical arena. Pope John Paul II describes the whole church as "a community of disciples" called to a difficult moral mission. Although immigrant U.S. Catholicism often resorted to an uncritical patriotism to refute nativist charges of divided loyalties,[6] the bishops warn that no automatic agreement can be presumed between the gospel and the American way of life:[7]

> We readily recognize that we live in a world that is becoming increasingly estranged from Christian values. In order to remain a Christian, one must take a resolute stance against many commonly accepted axioms of the world. . . . To set out on the road to discipleship is to dispose oneself for a share in the cross. *(CP,* 277, 276)

This witness will be countercultural because an increasingly militarized society will not likely welcome a church of peacemakers.

The third biblical theme states that the peace of Christ has been inaugurated but has not definitively arrived—that peace is "already . . . but not yet." In a world of sinful individuals and social structures, such as economic exploitation and bellicose nationalism, the promise of God's victory in Christ has not yet been fully realized. The church needs to hear both pacifists and just-war advocates since they witness to the dialectical tension

39

involved in peacemaking. *Already* we experience the reconciliation accomplished in Christ; on this the pacifist insists. The advocates of justifiable defense point to the other side of the truth: that because we live in a world of sin, the promise of peace is *not yet* fulfilled.

> We must continue to articulate the belief that love is possible and the only real hope for all human relations, and yet accept that force, even deadly force, is sometimes justified and that nations must provide for their defense. *(CP,* 78)

Despite this attempt at balancing the two groups, the bishops maintain that those who seek nonviolent means of resolving conflicts best express the example of Jesus *(CP,* 78).

The tension between the example of Jesus and the political conditions of force and violence is not resolved in the letter. Methodologically, the argument moves from the empirical situation to the Scriptures, only to be checked by a doctrine steadfastly maintained by the tradition and philosophical ethics: namely, the right to self-defense and the duty of leaders to defend their subjects.[8]

One wonders whether the tension between self-defense and the example of Jesus is not more extreme than the bishops envision. Does the right to self-defense have equal theological standing with the call to imitate the nonresistance and forgiving love of Christ?[9] Was that right developed during eras when the tradition largely ignored the biblical call to peacemaking?

The biblical theology of peace presented in the pastoral letter contributes a new perspective to the discussion among Christians. It opens up space to consider the fundamental theological beliefs behind the political proposals on all sides.[10] It makes pacifism a legitimate vocation in the church, in line with Vatican II but reversing Pope Pius XII's negative judgment on lay pacifism.[11] In addition, it links the question of peace to that of justice and forces us to look at the global arms race from the perspective of the poor.[12] Finally, the letter reminds us that the fundamental motivations for framing strict limits on the resort to force are the biblical concern for the neighbor (even if that neighbor is our enemy) and for the defenseless who require our aid. Both pacifists and just-war advocates start from the same premise: Do no harm to the neighbor. They can also concur on practical conclusions. *The Challenge of Peace* takes a just-war route to arrive at a position that is very close to nuclear pacifism.

The Morality of Nuclear Deterrence

In this section we consider the rationale for concluding that nuclear deterrence may be morally legitimate under certain strict conditions. First, we look at the just-war principles invoked in the argument. Second, we see how they apply to the novel situation of nuclear deterrence and U.S. strategic policy. Third, we examine the morality of the "conditional intention" to wage nuclear war that makes deterrence credible to the adversary. We move from the language of biblical faith to the broader categories of human morality in order to bring some moral clarity to the public debate.

Just-War Principles in a Nuclear Era

A fundamental question raised by pacifists is whether the traditional moral thinking about warfare is still legitimate in the

William C. Spohn, S.J.

era of nuclear weapons and strategies of mutually assured destruction.[13] Others have argued that however we think about warfare, we always come back to the categories and principles enunciated in the tradition of just-war thinking.[14]

The just-war tradition represents a 1600-year attempt to restrict the resort to violence under stringent conditions.[15] Its basic intention is no different from the ancient *lex talionis* of "an eye for an eye and a tooth for a tooth." This principle of rough justice attempts to limit violent retaliation, not to legitimize it: No one should demand two teeth for the loss of one. Although since the 16th century nation-states have often perverted the just-war theory by using it to legitimate their offensive wars, that abuse does not invalidate the original intention to limit the recourse to violence within moral boundaries.[16]

The Challenge of Peace presumes that the just-war doctrines can continue to illuminate moral choices in the nuclear era. It responds to the question of irrelevance by trying out the traditional principles of just-war thinking to see whether they are still adequate today. If they clarify the issue, they should not be dismissed as passé. We have to test the two sources of moral theology that support just-war thinking (i.e., ethics and tradition) against the new empirical data.

There are two sets of norms in the just-war tradition. The *jus ad bellum* norms limit the recourse to war (e.g., it must be in a just cause, declared by competent authority, only a last resort, etc. [*CP*, 85–99]). The *jus in bello* conditions, on the other hand, restrict conduct within war.

Since nuclear deterrence is based on the threat to retaliate rather than to inaugurate hostilities, the bishops do not consider the *jus ad bellum* criteria at any length. They hold that no nation has the right to initiate nuclear war under any circumstance.

The two conditions for the just conduct of war occupy their attention. First, the principles of discrimination:

> The lives of innocent persons may never be taken directly, regardless of the purpose alleged for doing so. . . . Just response to aggression must be discriminate; it must be directed against unjust aggressors, not against innocent people caught up in a war not of their making. *(CP,* 104. This is also known as the principle of noncombatant immunity.)

Second, they discuss the principle of proportionality:

> The damage to be inflicted and the costs incurred by war must be proportionate to the good expected by taking up arms. *(CP,* 99)

The bishops state that these principles are integral to human morality. They presume that these principles are universally authoritative, even though they do not expect universal agreement on the application of the principles. When we move to concrete applications we confront data on technical matters, the psychology of the adversary, the intricacies of global strategy, and the like, which may be interpreted differently by people of good will. Not everyone will agree with the bishops' recommendation against the first-use policy that underlies American strategy in Europe. Hence, while the bishops expect agreement on the principles, they propose their applications as less binding *(CP,* 9, 10).

William C. Spohn, S.J.

Nuclear Deterrence

Is it possible to invoke moral principles on the conduct of warfare to judge deterrence, which is a strategy designed to prevent war? By definition, deterrence is the policy of preventing one's adversary from initiating acts of aggression by threatening the adversary with retaliation that will cause unacceptable damage. Of all the moral dilemmas posed by the new conditions of nuclear strategy none is thornier than the question of deterrence. It appears to have contradictory elements:

> The paradox of deterrence is rooted in the fact that intention (nuclear war prevention) and action (the preparation and threat to unleash nuclear war) move in opposite directions. In order to achieve the goal of war prevention, deterrence policy threatens precisely what it seeks to avoid.[17]

How can we judge a policy that contains an intention that might never be carried out? That is, the threat of retaliation does not automatically mean that the U.S. would in fact engage in massive nuclear retaliation should the Soviets engage in nuclear aggression against us or our allies. The declaratory policy may be different from an actual policy known only to the nation's leaders. On the other hand, deterrence can only be effective if it is credible to the adversary. They must be persuaded of our willingness to carry out the threatened retaliation.

Deterrence, therefore, is an intention rather than an action. It is a policy whose ultimate intent is to forestall an action—namely, military aggression by the adversary. Since we can scrutinize the morality of intentions by examining the morality of what is intended, we can come to some moral judgment on the morality of our present deterrence policy. We do not have to wait until the intention is carried out to assess its moral quality. An intention to do moral evil corrupts the moral agent who has such an aim, even if circumstances prevent the agent from carrying it through. The basic premise of the argument seems obvious: If it is morally wrong to do *X,* it is morally wrong to threaten to do *X*—even though it may not be wrong to the same degree as the actual deed. The bishops make this premise explicit in their summary:

> No *use* of nuclear weapons which would violate the principles of discrimination and proportionality may be *intended* in a strategy of deterrence. The moral demands of Catholic teaching require resolute willingness not to intend to do moral evil even to save our own lives or the lives of those we love. *(CP,* iii–iv)

The *corruption of moral agents* is at issue here, whether or not the threat is ever carried out. For example, if I prevent you from committing murder by holding your children hostage, have I done the right thing morally? Although I am preventing murder, I am using blackmail to do it because I am using your children as pawns. This violates their human dignity and might cause lasting psychological harm to them. What does this threat do to me? I may be preventing murder, but do I become a blackmailer and kidnapper in order to prevent a "greater evil"? Some would argue that this example fails when we move from individual threats to relations between states, but it does highlight the moral cost of conditional threats.[18]

The key moral issue, therefore, in judging nuclear deterrence lies in what sort of retaliation is intended. Are we threatening to do something that would be morally wrong to do? The bishops do not state that every conceivable form of deterrence is immoral.[19] They do not endorse the present forms of

45

retaliation threatened by the superpowers. They reject any first resort to nuclear weapons, even to repel a conventional attack. Hence, they advocate a "no first use" policy in Europe, which would be a reversal of 40 years of NATO strategy *(CP,* 150–56). Both U.S. and Soviet strategies of nuclear response to nuclear aggression are morally deficient because "a nuclear response to either conventional or nuclear attack can cause destruction which goes far beyond 'legitimate defense' " *(CP,* 160). Because these strategies would be morally wrong to implement they would also be morally wrong to intend as part of a deterrence strategy.[20]

The pastoral letter invokes an argument from authority at this juncture. The bishops cite the teaching of Pope John Paul II to rescue some form of deterrence from the moral condemnation they had leveled at its present forms:

> In current conditions deterrence based on balance, certainly not as an end in itself but as a step on the way toward a progressive disarmament, may still be judged morally acceptable. Nonetheless, in order to ensure peace, it is indispensable not to be satisfied with this minimum, which is always susceptible to the danger of explosion. *(CP,* 173)[21]

Had the bishops ruled out all possible use of nuclear weapons, they could not have accepted nuclear deterrence in any form, since every conditional intention to use would have been linked to an action that was morally wrong. They allowed a "centimeter of ambiguity" regarding a valid use of nuclear weapons without specifying what that would be.[22]

There can be no confusion about their moral criticism of present U.S. and Soviet strategic planning. Their negative evaluation rests on the *jus in bello* criteria. The first is the principle of discrimination or noncombatant immunity. Total war is never justifiable since it directly attacks the innocent. Some might argue that targeting civilian populations for nuclear annihilation would be a more effective deterrent than merely targeting factories, military bases, and so on. However, that strategy would involve an immoral intention because the policy is deliberately indiscriminate.

Both Casper Weinberger, then defense secretary, and William Clark, then national security adviser, assured the bishops' committee that the U.S. "does not target the Soviet civilian population as such." Rather, the "war-making capability of the Soviet Union, its armed forces and industrial centers, were directly targeted for a retaliatory strike" *(CP,* 178 n. 81). Since many of these targets are located in proximity to large civilian populations, we must inquire what the indirect effect of such counterforce targeting would be. The U.S. strategy identifies 60 military targets within the city limits of Moscow alone and 40,000 military targets in the Soviet Union as a whole. The bishops concluded that nuclear strikes on such a scale would be morally disastrous: "The number of civilians who would necessarily be killed by such strikes is horrendous" *(CP,* 180).

Testimony by administration officials indicated that even though planners hoped to keep any nuclear exchange limited,

> they were prepared to retaliate in a massive way if necessary. They also agreed that once any substantial numbers of nuclear weapons were used, the civilian casualty levels would quickly become truly catastrophic, and that even with attacks limited to "military" targets, the number of deaths in a substantial exchange would be almost indistinguishable from what might occur if civilian centers had been deliberately and directly struck. *(CP,* 180)

In effect, one cannot judge the intentions of a policy by the language in which it is expressed. Whether public officials

47

call the targeting "counter-force" or "counter-population" is less relevant than the probable consequences of the policy. On that score, the morality of our present targeting policy is ambiguous at best.

When we turn to the second *jus in bello* criterion, that of proportionality, the issue becomes clearer. The extent of damage to civilians in the area of attack as well as those affected by radioactive fallout would be disproportionate to any political objectives sought by a retaliatory strike. Here it is important to note a key assumption the bishops felt constrained to make— no nuclear war could be kept limited for long:

> The technical literature and the personal testimony of public officials who have been closely associated with U.S. nuclear strategy have both convinced us of the overwhelming probability that major nuclear exchange would have no limits. *(CP,* 144)

The ensuing devastation would be so extensive that it could not be justified as a moral means to any objective. Putting the two criteria together, therefore, the bishops conclude that "such a strike would be deemed morally disproportionate, even though not intentionally indiscriminate" *(CP,* 182).[23] Therefore, if the plans are for an immoral action, the intention behind our present strategic policy is immoral. This conclusion should be intelligible to any reasonable person of good will and not only to believers.

What positive recommendations can be made for moving us from an objectively immoral situation of deterrence to one that begins to conform to the strict conditions described in the statement of John Paul II? Three moral norms would undergird any legitimate policy of deterrence:

> 1. If nuclear deterrence exists only to prevent the *use* of nuclear weapons by others, then proposals to go beyond

this to planning for prolonged periods of repeated nuclear strikes and counterstrikes, or "prevailing" in nuclear war, are not acceptable. . . .

2. If nuclear deterrence is our goal, "sufficiency" to deter is an adequate strategy; the quest for nuclear superiority must be rejected.

3. Nuclear deterrence should be used as a step on the way toward progressive disarmament. Each proposed addition to our strategic system or change in strategic doctrine must be assessed precisely in light of whether it will render steps toward progressive "disarmament" more or less likely. *(CP,* 188)

In light of these more proximate moral norms, the United States Catholic Conference has testified against the MX and Pershing II missiles and questioned the moral legitimacy of the Strategic Defense Initiative. In these testimonies the bishops have linked the expenditure on new weapons programs to the question of justice.[24] In the pastoral letter the bishops endorse a radical limitation of nuclear arsenals on both sides to the level of "sufficiency" to deter rather than the 50,000 nuclear warheads in place today. They also call for unilateral initiatives and serious negotiations on arms reduction, a prospect that seemed terribly remote in the bellicose early years of the Reagan administration *(CP,* 190, 191).

How Moral Is a Conditional Intention?

Much of the public reaction to *The Challenge of Peace* has focused on the issue of the conditional intention involved in nuclear deterrence. The most common criticism is that the letter is inconsistent because it joins moral condemnation of the foundations of any credible deterrence posture with limited moral toleration of deterrence in principle.[25]

Intentions, no less than positive actions, are the subjects of moral scrutiny. If someone intends to murder another but is only prevented from doing so by circumstances, that person is still morally blameworthy. When I intend to do an action under certain conditions, I am already increasing the likelihood that action will occur, even if it is an action morally reprehensible to me. Christians find the level of intention of special interest because Jesus' concern for the "heart" as the true origin of evil requires careful attention to motives and intentions.[26]

We need to examine *what* we intend in deterrence as well as *how* we intend it. I will accept for the sake of argument the conclusion reached by *The Challenge of Peace*—namely, that the present strategic plans for nuclear retaliation are both indiscriminate and disproportionate, hence grossly immoral. Can one intend any form of credible deterrence for the sake of preserving greater values, such as the defense of the democratic, capitalist way of life?

The issue of nuclear deterrence is thorny because it is unclear precisely *how* we maintain the threat. How do we hold the intention to retaliate on a massive scale of nuclear destruction? (1) Is it a threat that is virtually a bluff, namely, one we never intend to carry out? (2) Is it no bluff but an intention we fully intend to execute? (3) Or is it a "conditional intention," one that we are willing to carry out if and only if certain conditions are met? These three positions vary in moral seriousness since each poses a lesser or greater likelihood of acting on the intention.

I wish to strike the first two meanings of intention mentioned above. (1) Our present deterrence posture is clearly more than a bluff since its implementation appears to be assured by commitments both on the level of technology and personnel. (2) Our present deterrence posture does not directly intend to retaliate on a massive scale to Soviet aggression, but in the larger framework of the policy it intends to deter such aggression. We have no certainty that our actual policy would be as catastrophic as our declared policy.

Therefore we are left with the third meaning of intention. We have a conditional intention to retaliate on a massive scale, and that intention is clearly discernible to our adversary. Due to the logic of a "credible deterrence" the adversary can be deterred only if the adversary is convinced that our actual policy matches our declared one.

In a democracy the issue of credibility raises serious moral problems. Our leaders may be exonerated from holding an evil intention because they might never resort to the massive murder-suicide involved in nuclear retaliation should the Soviets launch a first strike. However, the majority of the populace must be convinced that such an immoral retaliatory strike can and should be launched. The leaders have the moral luxury of an actual policy at variance with the declared policy, while the population needs to be "willing" to have an immoral action performed in their name. Does this mean a credible deterrence policy in a democracy necessarily involves foisting on the populace an immoral intention that may erode their moral integrity?

Robert McKim probes the question of conditional intention and posits this thesis: "It is wrong to intend conditionally to do what is known to be wrong to do."[27] This clearly states the dilemma that lies at the heart of a conditional acceptance of nuclear deterrence in any credible form.

From both the right and the left the pastoral letter has been criticized on this precise point. Those who criticize can be divided into two main groups: those who argue against conditional acceptance of nuclear deterrence because it involves approving an intrinsically evil action, and those who argue against that acceptance because it leads to evil consequences. The critics choose different moral grounds to argue the same point: the weight of the bishops' condemnation of present forms of nuclear deterrence should have led to a condemnation of all forms of deterrence. The argument's momentum goes against the papal statement invoked to settle it. As David Hoekema expresses it:

> The pastoral letter argues so forcefully against important elements of nuclear deterrence that one is tempted to read it as a subtle kind of syllogism with a trick conclusion—an argument *against* nuclear deterrence into which a statement of approval has been grafted.[28]

Nonconsequentialist Criticisms

First, let us look at those who reject nuclear deterrence *in principle* and consider the political and cultural consequences of that rejection as morally irrelevant. Interestingly enough, both liberal pacifists and traditionalists agree on this issue. Both hold that an absolute moral value is violated by the threatened nuclear retaliation. For traditionalists that value is *innocent human life,* which can never be taken under any circumstances. The pacifists hold that *human life* as such is an absolute value that is inviolable.[29]

The traditional teaching of Roman Catholic moral theology that certain acts are intrinsically evil and can never be justified by favorable consequences underlies the traditionalist criticism. Russell Shaw writes:

> A conditional intention signals a state of will that is already morally good or evil, whether or not the conditions triggering the prospective behavior ever arise and the behavior

occurs. . . . We are morally responsible for the evil we will
to do (or, as with deterrence, that we will to be done on
our behalf). But we are not morally responsible for—guilty
of—the evil that is done to us, even though we may foresee
it as a consequence of our own ceasing to do evil.[30]

Because deterrence might fail, any conditional acceptance
of it must involve a willingness to use nuclear weapons. That
willingness is itself morally wrong. The loss of political auton-
omy, religious freedom, and so on, are not relevant considerations to balance off the morally evil policy of nuclear deterrence.
No intrinsically evil means may be used to achieve a good end.[31]

The Consequentialist Position

Most commentators on the letter are not persuaded by the
deontological claim that certain acts are intrinsically evil. While
they acknowledge the moral evil of nuclear retaliation, they do
not assert that any conditional intention to use nuclear weapons
as part of deterrence is wrong in principle. Rather, they balance
the risk of nuclear war against the values preserved by deterrence
and find either that there is a proportionate reason for justifying
some forms of deterrence or that there is no proportionate reason
for the risk and judge those forms morally unjustifiable. The
bishops themselves reflect traditional just-war thought when
they attempt to balance the call to do no harm with the obligation
to protect the innocent. They are unwilling to set aside either
of these competing but not irreconcilable claims: "The moral
duty today is to prevent nuclear war from ever occurring *and*
to protect and preserve those key values of justice, freedom and

William C. Spohn, S.J.

independence which are necessary for personal dignity and national integrity" *(CP,* 175).[32]

The consequentialist commentators hold that a policy cannot be evaluated by isolating the moral act implied in deterrence. The effects on one's family, fellow citizens, and citizens of other states must be taken into account as we debate what to do about deterrence. Moral evaluation cannot prescind from practical and prudential considerations. It may have been a grave moral error to have inaugurated the posture of mutually assured destruction, but that is not the issue the world faces at this point. Rather, we need to suggest how to move from the present situation, which I believe the bishops have shown to be an immoral form of deterrence on both sides, to a new position that comes closer to sanity and morality. Both pacifists and those who consider all deterrence an intrinsically evil act seem forced by the absolutist logic of their position into adopting unilateral disarmament. Such a move might be tremendously destabilizing as well as disastrous for the survival of key human values.[33] Unilateral initiatives toward disarmament, on the other hand, are morally imperative—but so is a strategy for gradual and progressive bilateral reduction of nuclear weapons of all sorts.

The authors of *The Challenge of Peace* avoided any decision between nonconsequentialism and consequentialism as a preferred mode of conducting ethics. Currently in Catholic moral theology a brisk debate is raging between traditionalists and "revisionists" over this fundamental question of method in ethics.[34] Although the letter assiduously avoids spelling out its methodology in any detail, it seems clear that the bishops did not endorse the position that any use of nuclear weapons would be intrinsically immoral.[35]

James W. McGray argues that the bishops' conditional toleration of nuclear deterrence can be supported on traditional Catholic casuistry, the principle of double effect, to offer a

54

rationale for their position.[36] He also asserts that the double-effect rationale justifies continued deployment of nuclear weapons for a while, the considerable risks notwithstanding. His rationale rests on four conditions: (1) "Continuation of the deterrence threat is not intrinsically immoral";[37] (2) the good effect of deterring nuclear war is directly intended; the bad effects, namely, the risks inherent in the threat, are not directly intended but regretfully tolerated as a side effect; (3) "The bad effects are not chosen as means to the good effects. The U.S. is not 'holding innocent people hostage' in order to deter their leaders from behaving immorally. Our weapons are only aimed at military targets";[38] and (4) "The good effects are commensurate with the bad effects." McGray acknowledges that this condition is the most problematic. "Given the potential for disaster, the fundamental moral imperative is to use the peace of a sort which we enjoy to work desperately to extricate ourselves from our nuclear-deterrence predicament."[39]

McGray has stated the dilemma inherent in just-war considerations of the morality of the conditional intention involved in deterrence. I would go a step further and agree with the critics that the limited toleration of deterrence expressed by Pope John Paul II does not follow from the argument of the pastoral letter. It is invoked as an argument from authority and doubtless served as a political compromise between just-warriors and pacifists in the U.S. Catholic hierarchy. I do not see how any form of deterrence could be both credible and moral.[40] The threat of a "sufficient" deterrent force of even 750 warheads per side would still appear to be disproportionate. By failing to propose some form of nuclear deterrent that would meet the criteria of discrimination and proportionality, the bishops weakened their case.

The committee of bishops that drafted *The Challenge of Peace* is currently evaluating subsequent developments in superpower relations in light of the letter's principles. One would

William C. Spohn, S.J.

hope that they would state with greater clarity whether such proposals as the Strategic Defense Initiative (SDI) meet moral criteria or in fact move us further away from the eventual elimination of nuclear weapons. "Star Wars," however, is not the most significant development in the three years since the letter was issued. Far more important is the change of official attitude toward the long-standing policy of mutually assured destruction (MAD). Although I believe that SDI is a technological illusion and could be a trillion-dollar assault on the poor, I believe that we owe former President Reagan some measure of thanks for articulating the growing public sentiment on the immorality of MAD.

Nuclear deterrence by the threat of massive retaliation is an idea whose time has come—and gone. The postwar moral consensus on strategic policy has unraveled in recent years.[41] That policy aimed to prevent two threats: that of Communist domination of the Western world, and the threat of nuclear war. For more than 30 years Communist domination was seen as the greater risk, but recently the danger of nuclear war has come to be judged the greater risk. President Reagan's remarks on MAD reflect this breakdown of confidence in nuclear deterrence.

Robert MccGwire of the Brookings Institute, formerly a senior military analyst for NATO, points out the nature of the change in priorities:

> We must . . . acknowledge that it is as important to dismantle the intellectual edifice we have erected over the past 30 years as it is to dismantle the structure of armaments we have built up during that same period. We need to recognize that the concept of deterrence is part of the problem and not the solution, and that the primary threat is war and not Soviet military aggression. And if the primary

threat is war, the way out of our defense dilemma will be found not in different military postures of force structures, although undoubtedly such adjustments will have to play a part, but in restructuring our assumptions.[42]

I believe that the U.S. bishops have contributed to dismantling the edifice of deterrence by showing the contradictions involved in it. They initiated a serious dialog between all parties to policy making in language that was not narrowly confessional and hence moved the moral concerns of believers more directly into the broader national debate. They attempted to move the administration away from dangerous bellicose rhetoric and plans for nuclear war fighting by questioning the moral legitimacy of our deterrent posture. Perhaps their discussion of the conditional intent involved in deterrence did not go far enough, but it did serve to dispel the myth that our strategic policy is or has been morally legitimate.

The sources of moral theology (Scripture, tradition, ethics, empirical data) are in principle complementary, but they also should be mutually corrective. The emphasis of the tradition on analyzing the moral act can be myopic if it is detached from the background of moral concerns and religious meaning. Perhaps the pastoral letter did not always keep the analysis of deterrence in the framework supplied by the biblical theology of peace and the urgent exhortations not to legitimate the idea of nuclear war. The tension between moral passion and patient moral analysis is always difficult to maintain. As Christians we are called to recognize that we exist under a dangerous occasion of sin and simultaneously to think as clearly as possible for ways to get beyond it. Perhaps then we will find a way to tear up the nuclear mortage under which we now exist.

The Just-War Legacy in the Nuclear Age

Paul Seabury

WE ADDRESS the question of the Christian faith and the problem of nuclear war in a century that has been tormented by two closely interwoven and novel developments. Both have profoundly challenged Christians and secular humanists whose abiding aspirations have been for a *tranquillitas ordinis*—a tranquil order in freedom, harmony, and peace.[1] These aspirations, which to some in the Victorian age seemed attainable if not inevitable, have been severely tested. The first terrifying setback was the eruption of what the late Raymond Aron termed "total war"—which twice has beset humankind in the first part of our century, before the appearance of nuclear weapons of today's enormous scale. The second, accompanying this, has been the advent of revolutionary totalitarianism with its widespread violence.

Intertwined in actual history, the two have acted to intensify each other. In combination, they have threatened the bases and core values of our Western civilization. But totalitarianism has not required war to consummate its ends. Even as war has taken its toll in lives and fortunes on a scale never before witnessed or imagined in history, Nazi and Communist totalitarianism, too, have exacted a heavy toll in human life and on the human spirit in both war and peace.

We need only recall the enormous peacetime casualties of defenseless peoples at the hands of totalitarian states. The number of people who perished, unarmed, at the hands of totalitarian movements and forces in the 20th century may greatly exceed the number of deaths in actual combat. Our memories, oddly, recall more readily the horrors of Hitler, Stalin, and Mao than the horrors more recently experienced in Southeast Asia by helpless people in peacetime, in Africa by unarmed peoples at the hands of dictators such as Haile Mengisto in Ethiopia, and by many others. Peace, if understood as the absence of armed conflict, can be as murderous as war in its effect upon human life, and can take its equally sinister toll in the subjugation of millions to ugly forms of servitude. When this kind of peace came to Cambodia in 1975, more Cambodians perished, defenseless and abandoned, than had been killed in 10 years of previous war. The administrative casualties of totalitarian regimes—whether in Auschwitz or the Gulag Archipelago—cannot be considered as consequences of war itself but as unpleasant features of peacetime.

The "boat people" of the 1970s and early 1980s, whether they have come from Vietnam, Cuba, or elsewhere, bear witness to the dangerous recourse some have taken to escape unendurable subjugation when the guns have become silent. Our understanding of the meaning of peace as the absence of actual organized combat must always in this century bear such possibilities in mind.

One of the ironic characteristics of war at all times, when we consider the relation of war and peace, is that those who choose to defend themselves, either by the posture of deterrence or by the willingness to take up arms against aggression, must face the charge of technical culpability for war. That is, in defending their values and their interests by obstinately resisting, these people share in the responsibility for war because, if they had surrendered without resistance, would there not have been peace? There would be peace today in Afghanistan if the resistance threw down its arms, as Soviet officials have suggested. The Christian view of war and peace must honestly confront these ambiguities of our times.

Nuclear and Conventional Deterrence

I introduce my thoughts on this general subject in this fashion in order to emphasize what should be apparent to anyone with a historical sense: These 20th-century experiences predate the atom bomb, just as they have continued to occur over us as real experiences on our planet. They hover over us as both real experience and future possibility. War can be quite total without them, regardless of the conditions. They powerfully remind us that our predicament cannot fix upon the relinquishment of some terrifying weapon—such as the nuclear one—in the quest for a peace that is more than the absence of armed conflict, and that should sustain our civilization. The conditions of peace-in-freedom cannot be won through fixation upon disarmament, arms control, or particularly upon unilateral renunciation or reduction. Our fixation upon nuclear weapons as a prime cause of international tension should not cause us to forget the real horrors of what some today nostalgically call "conventional war."

Some cynics, observing the 1987 negotiations for European-theater nuclear weapons withdrawal, argue that the aim or consequence of successful agreement will be to "make the world safe for conventional war." And to be sure, were nuclear weapons banned in Europe tomorrow, the democracies would face the choice between massive conventional rearmament or defenselessness. Matching the overwhelming, ever-growing Soviet superiority in conventional weapons so as adequately to deter aggression *in a nonnuclear mode* (were such politically accepted by Western publics) would require a Western arms mobilization of formidable proportions. The same moral questions raised today by Christians concerning "faith and weaponry" will continue to plague us under any form of arms regime, barring some unexpected and benign change in the political climate. Whether gestures of force reduction in nuclear weapons, or a principled abandonment of first use, or an announced renunciation of one-sided will to use would lead to a more safe or more problematic relationship among adversaries is hard to imagine. For those who regard deterrence today as a necessary though insufficient guarantor of peace and freedom, a charitable renunciation of it would be very problematic indeed.

I make this point neither from cynicism nor despair, but as a way of saying that the advent of nuclear weapons has not repealed either of the classic Christian traditions of the just war *(jus ad bellum* and *jus in bello)*. These traditions, stressing the principled criteria for resort to, and waging, war are as valid as ever before; and for Christians to jettison them simply out of fear of nuclear weapons (and their supposed disproportionality) leaves no alternative other than submission to the intentions of those with no similar compunctions. The Christian response to matters of war and peace cannot be reduced to the matter of the strategic management of Western nuclear arsenals or solely to the policies and strategies of the democracies. In the democracies, Christians, like all others, are free to offer their armchair or pulpit advice to troubled officials. In other less pleasant realms, Christians are imprisoned or murdered for raising these issues.

St. Augustine was first among those Christians who honestly sought to confront the harsh dilemmas that some theologians today seem to sweep under the rug. The abiding problem for him and others since him who share these concerns lies in the attempt to reconcile the Christian ethics of reconciliation, nonviolence, and forgiveness with Christian responsibilities within the cherished civic culture. Augustine sought to establish a valid ethic within an imperfect, mundane world. He explored the conditions that might offer the promise, if not the fulfillment, of an ordered and tranquil world under justice and law. He squarely faced the question of the place of force in the preservation of such a world. The renunciation of force in concrete situations was a problematical one, and it remains so. The role of force, specifically as deterrent to those who would disturb or destroy the peace, has long been of great importance. Thus, the New Testament was not a suicide pact.

The reconciliation of the Christian with transcendent expectations and hopes to a mundane and sinful world requires coming to terms with the relationship of force to a just society, and with the question of the criteria to which the Christian church should "direct the hearts and minds of Christian rulers." When Augustine wrote, the barbarians were already at the gates of his own imperfect civilization, and soon they were to overrun it. Could the Christians be accused of being, from conscience and principles, an objective accomplice to such a threat? Augustine greatly feared this; thus, his grand work. But, as some now would say, it was published too late. This is particularly ironic, given the rapid spread of the Christian faith in the late Roman era, when conversion was already a reality.

Paul Seabury

Can Nuclear War Be Just?

I notice now that some American theologians, not all of them Catholic, seek to erase Augustine's (and St. Thomas's) wise views of the idea of the just war. Nuclear weapons, they argue, have abolished their validity. Some of these theologians now feel it necessary for Christians to return to the purer instructions found in the New Testament alone. The argued logic of this view is that since the means of war now engulf the ends of war (thanks to nuclear weapons), the search for a new moral or just equation between the two is hopeless. The true Christian should stand free from the now outmoded, futile discussions about defense and deterrence, save to assert the preeminence of the value-free ethic of Christian nonviolence. To them, deterrence is ethically unacceptable (given the possible consequences of its failure, and given the evil intentions of use within it). The American Catholic bishops' advice on this portentous matter resembles that of those who might argue that police officers may carry pistols, on condition that they will never use them.

In the 1960s there was a rash of similar antinuclear protests in the West (such protests were ruthlessly repressed in the Soviet Union). Then, their symbolic leader was the English philosopher-mathematician Bertrand Russell. Roughly, Russell can be described as a secular humanist, and certainly not as a Christian. Like present-day advocates of unilateral nuclear disarmament, he too was convinced that the advent of nuclear weapons had abolished ordinary politics.

There was a harsh, consistent, apolitical logic in Russell's position. Before the Soviets acquired their own nuclear arsenal, Russell boldly supported American official proposals for an international ban on nuclear weapons. When the Soviets refused this well-meaning, if unrealistic, American proposal, Russell then called upon the Americans to issue an ultimatum: Comply, or else! (Needless to say, the Americans wisely did not take his advice.) But when the Soviets gained their own capability, Russell's logic led him to a different position: Because nuclear war is a grave threat to human life and the Soviets are obdurate and unwilling to forswear their own arsenal, the West—in the interests of human survival—should unilaterally disarm. Then there would be no nuclear war. Russell's logic was somewhat flawed—the only time when nuclear weapons *had* been used, in 1945, was when one side had them and the other did not. Yet Russell in his own way was more ruthlessly honest in the logic of his position than are some radical Christian theologians today. For him the logical question, starkly stated, arose from a concern for the survival of the human race. This should take precedence over the survival of any particular, or valued, part of humanity. The "bomb" had radically diminished the importance of ethical values. The necessary price of survival was submission, submission at least to those much less encumbered by moral considerations; and that meant submission to the totalitarians. It is no wonder that Russell's remarkable change of policy was welcomed in Moscow. The Committee on Nuclear Disarmament movement, which he symbolically led in his later years, was endorsed by Soviet propaganda.

The tendency of some American radical religious writers and church leaders in the 1980s to subscribe to Russell's bottom-line recommendations (advocating renunciation of nuclear first use and nuclear deterrence) rests upon reasons apparently different from Russell's, which were harsh biological ones. These "Christian" reasons ultimately are based upon radical precepts of nonviolence. (Oddly enough, consistencies here abound, since some of these radical advocates of nuclear nonviolence are those who now condone and even selectively support the use of violence in the name of liberation theology, and in the name of Marxist-Christian collaboration in the eradication of injustice.) No one, I would suppose, who is concerned either with biological or cultural survival lives easily with the strategic reliance of the Western democracies upon the terrifying logic of mutual assured destruction (MAD), or with its other names, nuclear stability or mutual deterrence (doctrines that the Soviets, apparently, in their quest for strategic superiority, do not seem to accept). These doctrines cause us great disquiet, and for obvious reasons. Yet their application to the main regions of East-West confrontation in the past 40 years has coincided with a long period of peace in those areas. In contrast, terrible wars have occurred in regions not covered by this strategic standoff. The many bloody wars around the world since 1945 have occurred in regions not blessed with Mutual Assured Destruction. That deterrence has worked in those realms does not mean that there is an ironclad law that it will continue to do so. If deterrence is an awesome basis for peace, and also imperfect, what might be a more wholesome substitute for it?

A Christian repudiation of nuclear deterrence, if such is conceivable, means little or nothing if it arises exclusively from a New Testament affirmation of moral motives as the primary justification of action. Those Christian scholars who have struggled with the practical questions of Reinhold Niebuhr's *Moral Man, Immoral Society* have necessarily been faced with the philosophical question of the relationship between moral intentions and real consequences. The American Catholic bishops, for instance, with their dangerously attenuated version of acceptable deterrence (in which the posture of deterrence remains, but the will of it is exorcised) have not advanced the discussion as to the necessary conditions for safety in freedom. I sleep better at night knowing that these bishops are not running the Pentagon.

One might think that those who shrink from the idea of the balance of terror as a permanent condition, or as a fallible one, would look with open eyes at more benign alternatives to MAD. One of them, and a morally attractive one at that, is the Strategic Defense Initiative. For all of its problematical difficulties, SDI presents a significant alternative to the balance of terror: It abandons the idea of countervalue and counterforce (the genocidal retaliatory destruction of whole cities or regions), substituting for it a doctrine based upon the defensive destruction of launched nuclear vehicles. It offers hope that the defense, rather than the offense, may be a viable means of conserving major civic and ethical values.

Strangely, however, many of those radical Christians who on spiritual grounds would dismantle the machinery of an immoral MAD reject SDI as well. What then would we have left? Perhaps they may be persuaded to look at this alternative again. In the meantime, I think that we should keep our eyes permanently on the issues of primary moral concern, the conditions for the survival of a culture within which Christian values may play a prominent role in an imperfect and very mundane world.

Abandoning the Just-War Legacy?

I now turn to the theological arguments of John Howard Yoder and William C. Spohn. If I understand them correctly—namely, their criticisms and revisions of Catholic perspectives on war and nuclear deterrence—they call for a drastic fundamentalism with far-reaching implications. I am not clear about the extent to which the thinking reflected in these two essays is shared within Christian thought. But according to one distinguished theologian, George Weigel, it appears widespread among many American Catholic theologians, other intellectuals, and professional staffers of religious organizations.[2]

This thinking proposes a scuttling of church moral teachings from the time of St. Augustine to the present—a scuttling that one might add has hardly been accepted by the Vatican.

Spohn reasons in this way:

> The argument here is addressed to those who believe in the God who speaks through the Scriptures. This treatment represents a significant advance [sic] over traditional Catholic discussion on war and peace since it presents a more historical notion of God.

The abandonment of church teachings, represented here as moral philosophy or natural law, clearly signifies in particular the abandonment of Catholic doctrines and teachings about the just war—doctrines that, incidentally, were precursors to modern *secular* international law, including the laws of war. There is more than a faint trace of Orwellian newspeak in Spohn's proposition that the abandonment or reduction of church doctrine and a *return* to scriptural fundamentalism represents an "advance"!

Something odd is going on here that is important to further argumentation. The abandonment of church teachings makes it possible to argue that Christ's followers, in imitation of him, should view their principal vocation as that of *peacemakers;* that the "ministry of reconciliation," particularly in a time of nuclear peril ("the cloud of nuclear extinction" prophesied by Carl Sagan, Helen Caldicott, and other apocalypts), must extend to the "sociopolitical arena of the superpowers." Since "reconciliation" is "at the heart of Christology," then all that doctrinally transpired between A.D. 300 and, say, 1985 or so, should be repealed or subjugated in favor of the Sermon on the Mount. Augustinian realism is dead. Operationally, in the "superpower sociopolitical arena," this means that America must drop its policy of strategic deterrence. *Christian* realism, also, is dead! Nonviolence now must be the centerpiece of Catholic thought on war and peace. It is almost as though the bomb has come as a benign *deus ex machina*.

In observing the draining of the tub of traditional Catholic teachings, it is not clear to me which is to be the baby, and which the bathwater. I shall return to this question.

The suggestion that Christians, concerned above all with peacemaking and reconciliation, should place themselves either above or between those who fight, or may fight, is an interesting suggestion. Propositions entailing that Christians imitate Christ and "resist not the evil one" are not new. They have long been found in some extreme Protestant sects—in the Quakers in particular; but they have not had a comfortable home in the Catholic church.

Such an assertion of Christian obligations imposes an ethic of perfectibility on ordinary persons, with·respect to individual behavior. Calling upon the Christian to *imitate* Christ is false. Such an imitation of Christ is not ethically possible for ordinary human beings in any age, even the nuclear one. As even Spohn notes with respect to Jesus' teachings, "He defended the rights of others but did not insist on his own." The elementary right of self-defense long has served those who cherish their own safety, their own freedom, their own secular culture, and even a Christian culture in a secular world.

The ethos of radical Christian pacifism—recommending the abandonment of self-defense—must be reexplored, even though it has long been discredited.

The ethos of extreme Christian pacifism may be morally permissible in the instance of some hypothetical person who has responsibility to no other persons. In all other cases, it is morally intolerable and foolish. It requires an immoral decision not to protect others who may face threat of attack.

69

Paul Seabury

One way to confront this pacifist position scripturally is to ask what Christ might have done had he been the Good Samaritan, coming on the scene earlier, when the thieves were assaulting their victim. Would he have forcefully defended the poor man, or would his moral presence have been sufficient to deter the thieves? Scriptures supply us with no answer; perhaps Christ's presence would have been sufficient, but we mortals are rarely endowed with divine talents.

To pursue this familiar theme further: Does one, as a mortal, abstain from defending one's family? One's friends? One's neighbors? One's own community? One's society? One's civilization? The ethic of absolute nonviolence suggests that nothing of value and no one of value are worth protecting if force is required. Pushed to its nuclear-age extreme, as Yoder and Spohn suggest, it means that using violence against attack should not be permitted.

Casuistry crops up in the Catholic bishops' theological discussions of deterrence holding that a temporary possession of deterrence *may* be morally permissible for their country, so long as there remains adamant refusal of use under any circumstances.

The perfectibility argument *(ahimsa,* we might say) is best made in the abstract, absent concrete circumstances and complications. But some advocates of *ahimsa*—nonviolence—in recent times have been more candid about its application in concrete instances. One was Gandhi.

Proffering free advice to persons and nations faced by mortal threats was an obsession of Gandhi in the 1930s and 40s. In the dark years of the late 30s and early 40s, Gandhi delivered profuse advice to the Free World on how to conduct its affairs in the face of Nazi aggression. His advice to European Jews, in 1939, was that they should allow themselves to be killed by the Nazis; this would set a profound example to the whole world.

70

After Hitler's conquest of France in 1940, Gandhi—through the British viceroy in India—wrote a desperate letter to the British people, urging them to surrender and suffer whatever consequences the Nazi invader imposed upon them. "Let them," he wrote, "take possession of your beautiful island with your many beautiful buildings. You will give all these, but neither your souls nor your minds." Churchill thought otherwise.[3]

"Resist not the evil one"—this scriptural admonition evidently was an occasional recourse of Gandhi. In December 1941, when Hitler's armies had commenced the extermination of undesirable races, Gandhi wrote a special letter to Hitler beginning with the salutation "Dear Friend." Gandhi sought then to recruit Hitler to *ahimsa*! The Fuhrer, the mahatma wrote, should now embrace all humanity "irrespective of race, color, or creed." Hitler did not trouble to reply.[4]

More can be learned from history. When Christianity converted Rome and overthrew paganism, the line between Christianity and Caesar became blurred. Now, Christians could become Caesars! Christians became a respected civic part of the Roman *res publica*. They thus became less ultramundane and more interested in the destiny of what Augustine of Hippo came to call the City of Man, as distinguished from the City of God.

Rome was sacked by Vandals in 410, and dark premonitions of the collapse of civilization began to enter peoples' minds. Pagans accused Christians of bringing about this perilous state of affairs. Christian scriptural injunctions were now undermining the walls of Rome! Small comfort to Romans were the promises of afterlife when this world was under profound attack by barbarians! To Augustine, in his *City of God,* fell the self-imposed task of reconciling the Scriptures with reality.

It is said by Yoder, in accordance with Scripture, that Christ came into the world not only as herald and rabbi, but as liberator. But in Augustine's Rome, what now does the liberator do when

Paul Seabury

he has far more than a foothold in "this world"? Are his liberated zones now worth defending? Should the foreign policy of a now Christianized Rome, assaulted by unfamiliar outside forces, be one of *ahimsa?* Could unilateral disarmament be the strategy for the survival of a now-established, far-from-perfect, Christian *polis?* Scriptures offered little advice as to this matter. In "this world," should Christian citizens be instructed to suffer conquest, and even martyrdom, even as they posed as reconcilers and peacemakers? Augustine's *City of God* addressed this matter realistically. Augustine advocated that a Christian polity should exist in an imperfect, mundane world and before the coming of the transcendental one—the *tranquillitas ordinis.* It required the Christian to defend the Christian realm. (An important codicil to this very unutopian Augustinian view was that Christians *by their own efforts* could neither advance nor consummate the coming of utopia or the coming of Christ.)

The Ultimate Value: Peace or Freedom?

No Protestant or Catholic can quarrel with the claim that Christians are to be peacemakers and reconcilers, but the heretical assumption that this should be the *overriding,* supreme obligation is questionable. The proposal that the Christian should be supremely devoted to the task of "being in between"—that is, being between those who fight and always concerned with the prevention or the suspension of all forms of violence—is a most peculiar view of things. The admonition, in its extreme form, extends even to situations in which Christianity itself is under assault. In Nazi Germany, this admonition would have been applied to the Catholics who fought against Nazism. The courage of such great German Catholic prelates

72

as Cardinal Faulhaber of Munich sprang from their conviction that Nazism was fundamentally evil and should be resisted. The Soviet Union, where Christians today and for decades have been ruthlessly persecuted, presents a contemporary illustration of this age-old problem. The present pope himself has been quite clear on this matter. "Pacifist declarations," he has said, frequently cloak plans for "aggression, domination, and manipulation of others," and could "lead straight to the false peace of totalitarian regimes." The potent use of threats of mass slaughter, for coercing those who have disarmed, remains the true nightmare of the West.[5]

There is such a reality as "false peace"—a cardinal element in the Catholic tradition, which revisionists do not seem to appreciate. The peace of which Augustine spoke, the *tranquillitas ordinis,* was the ordered harmonious existence of Christians within a just civic polity. That this civic peace should be treasured, when found, is the reason that church tradition has endorsed for centuries the *possibility* of a just war—a war resorted to in order to protect the conditions of civic justice and tranquillity.

It seems to me that the issue posed in this exchange of theological ideas is whether the advent of nuclear weapons can be used as an irrefutable argument for the abandonment of Catholic positions on the just war. Spohn, Yoder, and I seem to have no fundamental disagreement as to the ominous features of the nuclear problem. I am sure they and I would not disagree either as to the future possibilities of other "unconventional" weapons, such as chemical-bacteriological ones. I am sure that they and I can agree that there is no way in which the nuclear genie can be put back in its bottle. I am sure that they and I would not disagree as to the formidable possibilities of a large-scale future "conventional", non-nuclear war between or among the advanced nations.

73

Perhaps they and I may agree that since this world has known many devastating wars since 1945, inflicting huge casualties upon innocent victims in Asia, Africa, and the Middle East; and that war in general has not been repealed because of the advent of nuclear weapons. War has been a profoundly important means of coping with serious matters of state—as the Soviets' Afghan war illustrates. I would hope that they and I could agree that many forms of warfare today—particularly the many offensive proxy wars now being waged by the Soviet Union and its proxies in Africa and Central America—represent a kind of struggle that may continue indefinitely and present a serious problem for Western civilization.

Given all of these possibilities, it seems to me that the missing element in their arguments for unilateral disarmament is the one I have sketched out above. A Christian view of the problem of war and peace in this very imperfect world must necessarily and always address the twin questions of war and human freedom. George Weigel has recently written in the tradition of Niebuhr and John Courtney Murray:

> The Catholic tradition of moderate realism has persistently taught that war is not inevitable, only likely. . . . Catholic incarnational humanism stands firm in its acknowledgment of human propensities for evil. But it stands equally firm in its insistence that, even under the effects of original sin, we remain the image of God in history, creatures capable of hearing and responding to a divine word of invitation and challenge. That conviction is the ultimate basis of the Catholic heritage of *tranquillitas ordinis.* . . . We have been created for peace and freedom; peace and freedom now stand under mortal threat.[6]

I end with my opening theme: Christians must accept the reality and the challenge of the "two horsemen" of our times—

total war and totalitarianism. Our democratic world has been free of internecine state-to-state war for at least a century and a half. No democracy has fought another democracy since 1815. The wars we have fought, to defend our freedoms, have been defensive wars against others. Our problem, then, in a conflictual world with "others" is: How can we sustain a vigorous open world that is under siege?

In our troubled times the formula of strength and defense has been called containment. There may not be a better word to describe a defensive posture designed to keep the expansion of Soviet power in check. In the nuclear realm, the handmaiden of containment has been strategic deterrence. Yet the struggle remains a political one in which the steadfastness of the West has been tested again and again.

Comment

John C. Bennett

PUBLICATION OF SUCH clear and competent statements of these three approaches to the relation between Christian faith and the possession and use of nuclear weapons is a very great help to all of us who are struggling with that fateful and baffling issue. John Howard Yoder has done more than I have known a person of his absolutist convictions to do in relating his contribution to the thinking of others who take steps toward some of his conclusions from pragmatic or "realistic" presuppositions. William Spohn deals with the ethics of deterrence starting with the same criteria of the just-war tradition represented by the American Catholic bishops but pushes the argument to a more complete theoretical rejection of nuclear deterrence. Paul Seabury presents the prevailing, almost official view of nuclear deterrence and of the possible use of nuclear weapons to defend our values, and he does so in a way that forces those of us who have more in common with Yoder or Spohn to face issues that we prefer to neglect.

Yoder's own absolute pacifism with its implications for the possession and use of nuclear weapons is familiar, but he goes beyond most pacifists in welcoming support from those who on other grounds come close to his rejection of the use of nuclear weapons and of nuclear deterrence. I prefer in this context, instead of using the word "pragmatic," to speak of "consequentialists" who come to results in their thinking where they must say no for reasons that are really deontological. This would

77

be true of the initiation of the nuclear stage of a war, of "first use" of nuclear weapons. It would be true of the use of nuclear weapons against populations as people whom God loves and who are truly like us. Behind the "no" is the love of enemies, but really of people, most of whom are enemies only in a particular context for which they have little responsibility. I am interested that Yoder recognizes the way in which consequentialist considerations and deontological considerations are mingled in the same persons in the same areas of discussion.

My own thinking moves almost all the way with that of Spohn. He begins with the peace pastoral of the Catholic bishops. He seeks to draw the bishops away from their conditional acceptance of nuclear deterrence. Whether the bishops make this concession to deterrence as a compromise among themselves or in deference to Pope John Paul II, who makes a similar concession to deterrence, I do not know. It must be remembered that the French and German Catholic bishops continue to support the nuclear strategy of their governments. Can it not be said that the American bishops do reject deterrence in all cases that are expected or planned? They reject the deterrence involved in the option of "first use" so important to NATO and supported by our government. They reject deterrence involved in the threat to bomb populations. They reject deterrence involved in counterforce deterrence planned by our government with its thousands of targets in the Soviet Union, including many in Moscow. The correspondence between the bishops and our government's representatives quoted in Spohn's essay seems to me to be definitive in ruling out even a counterforce strategy. The Methodist bishops in their pastoral letter go beyond the Catholic bishops in emphasizing the effect of a nuclear war on the atmospheric and earthly environment, on creation itself. I believe that this is a very important addition to the usual teaching about noncombatant immunity in the "justifiable-war" tradition. The use of our own nuclear weapons may seriously damage our own life-support systems as well as those of our enemies. There is the danger that the escalation of nuclear war would not only victimize the people of the nations that have had no part in the conflict but also end human history. Often the talk is that our survival is at stake. It is even more important to say that for the political and ideological calculations of a few people in the superpowers of one generation to make it impossible for new generations to be born on this earth would be the greatest sin against both God and the humanity that God loves.

Theoretically, the Methodist bishops do reject deterrence totally, but it is interesting that neither their letter nor that of the Catholic bishops calls for unilateral nuclear disarmament. This means that both allow for a period in which possession of nuclear weapons by our country would remain a deterrent, perhaps an undeclared deterrent. Whatever the intention, this is a concession to what is politically possible. It is a safe guess that no politician who called for unilateral nuclear disarmament could be elected to national office.

Paul Seabury reminds us of realities many of us are inclined to forget and of dilemmas everyone must face, from which there is no good escape. His own apparent optimism that nuclear war can be kept limited and his assumption that freedom and the values of our society can be defended by the use of nuclear weapons raise the most important questions—more about them later.

Conventional war, especially with no moral inhibitions about bombing populations, was a great horror during World War II before the dropping of the atomic bomb. The bombing of Rotterdam and of British cities by the Germans, and the bombing of Dresden and of Japanese cities by our side raised as profound moral problems in terms of immediate casualties as the use of nuclear bombs for Christians and humanists. More

powerful nuclear bombs in terms of immediate casualties may
have only a quantitative difference, but there is a difference in
kind between conventional war and nuclear war in delayed effects on the atmospheric and earthly environment, in the long-
term destruction of the support systems for human living. I see
no indication that Seabury takes account of this difference. It is
this difference that leads me to say that among the surest victims
of the almost inevitable escalation of nuclear war would be the
institutions of freedom. The first necessities would be order and
coercive measures to put the resources for living together again.
The possibility of recovering the particular values of our society
that we treasure most would be at risk.

Seabury also makes the common mistake of regarding totalitarian communism as a monolithic and unchanging hostile
power. There are many forms of change in communism, not
least in Soviet communism since the death of Stalin. The eastern
European nations today in varying degrees are benefiting from
changes in the Soviet Union. The whole contrast between being
"red" or "dead" is false rhetoric. There are many shades of red
in the world today—ranging from, at one extreme, the Italian
Communist Party to the regime in North Korea at the other.
We still preserve in this country an unchanging anticommunism
that is a major source of confusion in American political thinking, though our government has varying relations with China,
Poland, Hungary, the Soviet Union, and Cuba.

Seabury accuses the bishops and Spohn of departing from
the Christian wisdom of the just versus unjust war tradition. I
think that he is wrong in this. They use that tradition to show
that the use of nuclear weapons would be unjust. The bishops
do so now in all expected situations and Spohn extends that
view to all situations. The great dilemma is created by the
marginal possibility that the possession of nuclear weapons may
deter their use by others and thus prevent nuclear war. The

bishops agree tentatively and conditionally on this for the immediate present, but this goes against the main thrust of their letter. The fact that Seabury emphasizes, as I do, that in all expected situations they deny the use of nuclear weapons must in the not-too-long run undercut the structure and credibility of deterrence, in which Seabury places his hope for peace. My hope for peace, as between the superpowers at least, comes from the growing realization in both of them that they cannot use their nuclear weapons without threatening their own environmental life supports. Christians, among others, must add that the superpowers cannot use their weapons without threatening the life supports of uninvolved neighboring countries in the northern hemisphere and perhaps beyond. Concern for the effects of a war on uninvolved nations greatly extends the range of the concept of noncombatant immunity.

I am surprised that Seabury regards SDI as a moral alternative. From what we know of it the idea of its providing a shield for the nation, a hope which guided President Reagan, is an illusion. Most likely it might be able to protect some of our weapons and control centers and become a threatening aspect of deterrence. We know now that the other side regards it as extremely provocative and its main effect may be to prevent more solid measures that may make the world safe, such as a drastic reduction of strategic weapons, followed by a similar reduction of conventional weapons.

I shall conclude this comment by making two supplementary suggestions: (1) the role of absolute pacifism and (2) the relation between those of us whose thinking is in line with that of either Yoder or Spohn and political decision makers in the United States.

First, pacifists often resent as patronizing suggestions by nonpacifists concerning the value of their vocational contribution. I do not regard absolute pacifism as a self-sufficient approach to national policy. Governments are trustees for the security of nations, and no powerful nation is pacifist in conviction, though it may be led to favor drastic changes in regard to the possession or use of nuclear weapons. The Catholic bishops go very far as nuclear pacifists, but as nonpacifists as a group they advise NATO to increase its conventional military capacity in order to have an alternative to the use of nuclear weapons. I finally came to the conclusion that the use of military force against Hitler's Germany was justified. Even Dietrich Bonhoeffer, who had been inclined toward pacifism, found himself praying for the defeat of his country because he saw no other way of its being delivered from Hitlerism. Terrible as were the immediate consequences of World War II, Europe, including Germany, was saved from Nazi domination. Japan was saved from its militaristic ethos to the benefit of itself and Asia. Defeated nations were helped to rebuild by the victors, partly to win their support against the Soviet Union. I doubt now, as I did in the 1940s, if there was a viable pacifist political alternative to military resistance.

The pacifist witness inside and outside the church has at least two roles of immense importance. It provides a continuous criticism of the "lesser evil" emphasized by nonpacifists. Lesser evils gain great momentum. They often become more evil. They generate their own defenses, and the power of the state is often used to threaten dissenters. The pacifist vision and vocation make possible a freeing perspective that no one else is likely to provide.

Stanley Hoffman of Harvard, who is a morally sensitive expert on foreign policy, puts the situation very well. In an essay on "The Political Ethics of International Relations" he says the following: "It is hard to imagine a statesman who does not seek to evaluate consequences and whose decisions are made without reference to the context, but there is of course a constant danger of ditching or diluting principles and slipping into mere opportunism when consequences (which are in any case hard to foresee) and context become the dominant considerations."[1] Since pacifists represent absolute principles they are in a better position than most other citizens to call the attention of world leaders and their agents and supporters to cases of "slipping."

Also, the pacifist is able to concentrate on nonviolent forms of resistance to any imposed regimes that might deny freedom and justice. Who else can provide leadership for such resistance? Today the mainline church, both Catholic and Protestant, accepts Christian pacifism as one persuasive interpretation of the implications of the teachings and example of Jesus for the vocation of Christians. This has not been clearly true until our time. In this respect both Vatican II and the peace letter of the American Catholic bishops are of great importance. Ecumenical Protestants gave this status to Christian pacifism at the Oxford Conference on Church, Community and State in 1937, one of the major events that prepared the way for the World Council of Churches.

In connection with nonviolent resistance to imposed controls by another power, is it not probable that the opportunities for this would be greater after a conventional military defeat than after a nuclear exchange that might be initiated in the name of defense of freedom? After such a nuclear exchange, it is doubtful that anyone could claim to be the winner, and any degree of escalation of the use of nuclear weapons would add uninvolved neighboring nations as victims.

Second, those who hold the views that Yoder, Spohn, and I have expressed cannot expect American political leaders to use the same language. Those who run for office will be on their guard against being regarded as soft on defense or not sufficiently anticommunist, though I have hope that most of the public will soon become more discriminating on the issue of communism. Our political leaders cannot be expected to renounce deterrence in principle, but it may be possible to choose leaders who will accept the idea of minimal deterrence as advocated by Robert McNamara and Admiral LaRoque. So far, chiefly elder world leaders have had the courage to lead in that direction. There will be a chance to choose political leaders who, while on their guard against familiar attacks on weakness in foreign policy, will move the country far away from its present nuclear militarism and from the present tendency to be governed in foreign policy by an unchanging anticommunism and an East-West view of the world's problems.

The opportunity of most Americans and especially our political leaders, who are vulnerable to criticisms for their being weak on defense or naive about the real nature of communism or of Soviet power, to move away from the assumptions of the cold war depends on the reliability of the changes that have already begun in our relations with the Soviet Union. It is significant, in view of his past anticommunist stance and his hostility toward the Soviet Union as the "evil empire," that President Reagan eventually said our relations with the Soviet Union have never been better.

I shall now call attention to two developments within the Soviet Union that provide hope for the end of the cold war. The first is a neglected aspect of the thinking of Mikhail Gorbachev. Everyone knows about his desire to restructure the Soviet economy, but for some this is seen merely as an effort to make the Soviet Union stronger, with the possibility that it may become a greater threat to the West. What is neglected is his thinking about the nature of the world, which is most completely expressed in chapter 3 of his book, *Perestroika*.[2] The second development in the Soviet Union that I shall emphasize is the gradual erosion among the Soviet people of their ideological commitment to the transformation of the world for the sake of communism. Insofar as this erosion has taken place there has been preparation for Gorbachev's vision of the world. The experience of *glasnost* has revealed results of decades of this ideological erosion.

The first is a coherent body of teaching about international affairs which, before the publication of Gorbachev's book, was expressed in a speech to an international audience in Moscow in February 1987. He appealed to "universal moral and ethical standards." He put great emphasis on "mutual security." He made it clear that no nation should use nuclear weapons. He said that there would be "no Noah's ark for a nuclear deluge." He followed up these ideas in the chapter to which I have referred in *Perestroika* entitled "How We See the World Today."

He quotes a neglected side of Lenin. He said of Lenin "that more than once he spoke of the priority of interests common to all humanity over class interests" and that it is "only now that we have come to comprehend the entire depth and significance of these ideas. It is they that are feeding our philosophy of international relations, and the new way of thinking."[3] He says, after outlining traditional Marxist thinking, which was limited to the emphasis on class conflict: "But now, with the emergence of mass, that is, universal destruction, there appeared a limit to class confrontation in the international arena: the threat of universal destruction. For the first time ever there emerged a real, not speculative and remote, common human interest— to save humanity from disaster." He denies that Marxists have "found the final truth" and says that "we have no intention whatsoever of converting everyone to Marxism." The new political thinking can, and must, "imbibe the experience of all peoples and ensure the mutual enrichment and confluence of various cultural traditions."[4]

The uncertainty about the length of Gorbachev's tenure as the Soviet leader causes me to speak of the second development in the Soviet Union, the erosion of commitment to the absolutistic communist ideology. It has prepared the way for Gorbachev and its results may survive him. It breaks out into the open in the experience of *glasnost,* which has given freedom to Soviets to seek without intimidation for truth that transcends any absolute ideology. One aspect of this freedom is expressed in Gorbachev's admission that the Soviet Union has been wrong in its repression of the church and of believers.

Robert Kaiser, former Moscow correspondent for the *Washington Post,* has written in his much-admired book that "of the intellectuals I knew, most agreed that a few people still believed passionately in the ideology but only a few."[5] Professor Robert Tucker, director of the Russian Studies Program at Princeton University, says that "the Communist myth no longer sustains more than a small minority, if that." He says of the people in the Soviet Union that they "*en masse* have stopped believing in the transcendent importance of a future collective condition called 'communism,'" that "they have stopped believing in the likelihood of the society arriving at that condition and in the desirability of trying to achieve it through the role of the Communist party."[6]

The erosion of ideological absolutism devoted to world revolution does not mean that the Soviet Union as a great power might not have expansionist goals that its neighbors and rivals may regard as a threat, but it does mean that such goals are more likely to remain limited than when a nation is inspired by a passionate sense of mission. Its people are more likely to give a high place to the goals of private life, among other things the shortening of the lines at stores, everyday economic security, and resistance to the reckless sacrifice of their children in war, not to speak of the risk of nuclear destruction of their nation. The motive for world domination ascribed to them by many Americans would have been undercut.

Under these circumstances the American people and their political leaders may come to deal with the Soviet Union as people whose aspirations are not different from our own (as began to be the case when they saw the Soviet people on television during the Moscow summit). They will be better able to move away from the militaristic distortion of our national life and culture.

Above all, in the context of the problems of nuclear ethics discussed in this volume, the distance between religious leaders who reject the use of nuclear weapons and our political leaders who are accountable for national defense may be narrowed. We may yet see light on the issues that divide the authors in this book.

Comment

George Weigel

THE 1983 PASTORAL letter of the National Conference of Catholic Bishops, *The Challenge of Peace*, was a historical benchmark in the ongoing debate among and within American religious communities on the relationship between Judeo-Christian moral norms and the choices faced by public officials in the arena of nuclear weapons policy. That debate had been under way since the late 1940s; it had ebbed and flowed in intensity, reaching a particularly high level of controversy in the early 1980s, the period during which the "nuclear freeze" proposal was enthusiastically promoted by many church agencies. But *The Challenge of Peace*, whatever its flaws of analysis and prescription, seemed to put the issue of morality and nuclear strategy on the public agenda in an unprecedented manner.

No longer, in the policy world, would issues of nuclear weapons policy be deemed to have merely strategic, technological, and political dimensions. It was now widely understood that there were questions of "ought" that had to be engaged, amidst the complex questions of "is." Getting that understanding nailed down in the policy community was no mean achievement; it was, I would argue, the principle achievement of *The Challenge of Peace*.

So the question before us, as we face these unavoidable issues between now and the turn of the millennium, is not *whether* there shall be moral argument about nuclear weapons and strategy. The question is *how*: With what wisdom shall the

American religious community help shape the debate over these weapons of unprecedented destructive capability? Will the debate within the policy community, narrowly construed, be more or less thoughtful because of the religious community's intervention? Will the nuclear weapons policies decided upon in our democracy make war more, or less, likely?

Things have changed in the years since *The Challenge of Peace* was published. The Reagan administration's Strategic Defense Initiative fundamentally altered the strategic and political debate by challenging the dominant orthodoxies of deterrence-plus-arms-control theory—even if many in the religious community (and in the policy community, for that matter) haven't quite caught up with that fact. The U.S./Soviet agreement on the elimination of intermediate-range nuclear weapons, and the widespread expectation of a follow-up agreement involving perhaps as much as a 50 percent reduction in strategic nuclear forces on both sides, has also altered the policy calculus and the public debate. The issue is no longer whether we shall have nuclear arms reduction agreements, but how these agreements shall be crafted so that they promote strategic stability and the pursuit of peace. Looking just down the road, one can imagine that, in the 1990s and because of European, Chinese, and Japanese concerns, the "linkage" between nuclear and conventional arms reductions will have to be remade, which will again pose a severe challenge to the court theologians of arms control theory, who have insisted for over a generation that such linkage be avoided.

So the strategic and political picture has made *The Challenge of Peace* not so much obsolete as historically contingent in a way that was perhaps hard to imagine during the drafting process in 1982 and 1983. How have others picked up the mantle of argument, in this new situation?

I am not enthusiastic about the United Methodist Bishops' letter, *In Defense of Creation,* which is perhaps the most developed post–*Challenge of Peace* statement by a major American denominational leadership. Aside from its failures to account for the changed strategic and political environment, *In Defense of Creation* suffers from a theological flaccidity that ought to be of serious concern. Most disturbing was the Methodist bishops' seeming endorsement of survivalism, a secular/New Age current in the freeze culture of the early 1980s that is rather at odds with Wesleyan theological intuitions. As Professor Stanley Hauerwas of Duke University (himself a pacifist) put it, "In a Jonathan Schell-like maneuver, the bishops seem to buy into the contemporary humanistic assumption that if death is the end not only of the individual but of the human species, all life loses its meaning. That, of course, is a form of atheism that one can only hope the bishops unintentionally and unreflectively proposed."

Hauerwas is, obviously, not one to mince words, and his summary indictment of the Methodist letter makes the crucial point:

> I think it is indicative of [the bishops'] failure to wrestle with the fundamental theological issues at stake in addressing the issue of nuclear war that *In Defense of Creation* spends much more time with the strategic and policy issues than with the theological. . . . One has the sense that in spite of their disavowal of being experts about nuclear strategy, the bishops feel more comfortable condemning SDI than they do in proclaiming God's sovereignty over our existence. [The bishops'] lack of theological reflection in *In Defense of Creation* is but an indication that they were more interested in the influence they might have in wider society than the stance the church as such should take.

"The stance the church should take"—that, it seems to me, is the nub of the question right now. It is a question that provides

91

the subtext for the Yoder, Spohn, and Seabury essays, but it is too rarely engaged directly, in this volume or in the general debate among religiously serious people. In short, the fundamental issues for the next stage of the morality-and-nuclear weapons debate are theological.

A brief anecdote may illustrate this. At the first meeting of the Catholic bishops' drafting committee, then–Archbishop Bernardin said that the committee would explore the full range of policy options but would in no circumstances endorse unilateral nuclear disarmament. Well, one wants to ask, why not? If the bishops were engaged in a serious exploration that began with Christian moral understandings and moved from there to policy prescriptions ("prudential judgments"), then why was the policy option of unilateral disarmament ruled out from the beginning? Or was it in fact the case, as I would argue, that the bishops' principal focus all along was the policy debate, wherein the very notion of unilateral disarmament is regarded as a sign of mental incompetence? In short, what the bishops did was foreclose the moral argument because of their concern that they be taken seriously in the policy debate. I am no supporter of unilateral disarmament, to be sure, but the bishops' procedure seems to me to have been precisely backward. Politics drove theology. So much for evangelical freedom.

The first order of business, then, in carrying on this essential argument is to get the priorities straight. Yoder's comment in the discussion, that God is responsible for history, not us, points in the right direction, although Yoder's formulation strikes me as insufficient.

Yoder is quite right to insist on the sovereignty of God over history. Moreover, one might argue in the face of the survivalists (Methodist and secularist) that Christians believe the worst in history has already happened. It took place on Good Friday and God's definitive answer to that radical evil was given on Easter Sunday. The eschatological horizon that bounds Christian hope relativizes all of our pretensions, and most especially our political and world-historical pretension. We are not "responsible for history" in the ultimate sense. But what about in a proximate sense? Does affirming the sovereignty of God over creation and history leave Christians in the position of Alfred E. Newman, that is, standing on the sidelines wearing a dumb grin and saying, "What, me worry?"

Yoder would not argue that, of course, and neither would the main currents of two millennia of Christian social ethics. We are not ultimately responsible *for* history, but we are responsible *in* history, because it is in history that we are called to the responsible exercise of neighbor-love. Thus there is no contradiction between affirming that Christian life is lived against and toward an eschatological horizon, and affirming that Christians are responsible for the shaping of history according to the moral norms they derive from their religious and rational convictions. Eschatology and moral responsibility is a both/and, rather than an either/or, matter.

Pope John Paul II caught this well during his 1987 visit to Uruguay and Chile. Asked, on the flight to Montevideo, whether he would not be "interfering in politics" in Chile, the pope said, "Yes, yes, I am not the evangelizer of democracy, I am the evangelizer of the Gospel. To the Gospel message, of course, belong all the problems of human rights, and if democracy means human rights it also belongs to the message of the church." The sequence is crucial here. First, the pope suggests, the church is the church, not a political lobby ("I come as the evangelizer of the Gospel"). Then the gospel is neither privatistic nor quietistic ("To the gospel message, of course, belong all the problems of human rights"). And in this world as it is, human rights are affected, for good or for ill, by the structures of political life (". . . and if democracy means human rights it also belongs to the message of the church"). Religious conviction · yields moral norms, which are then applied to questions of the right ordering of our lives and loyalties in human society. Theology is before politics, but theology does not absolve one from political responsibility.

The pope's brief statement is also useful in that it points us to an issue that was not adequately explored in this volume, namely, What is the peace that we seek in this world? Paul Seabury's essay is the only one that addresses this in any detail. Both Seabury and I agree that the classic Christian definition of peace is *tranquillitas ordinis,* an Augustinianism that I translate into modern terminology as "dynamic and rightly ordered political community." Peace, in this world, is not a matter of sentiment or will alone; peace is a matter of the structures of public life, within and among nations.

Viewed from this angle, the nuclear weapons debate is placed in its proper context. The fundamental moral issue in the war/peace debate is not the weapons themselves, but the anarchy of world politics. In other words, the weapons are the symptom, not the disease. A too-exclusive focus on symptoms can lead to a foreshortening of attention to the disease. Moreover, an apocalyptic rendering of the nuclear dilemma (as in the Methodist bishops' letter) can blind us to other symptoms that must be addressed if the world is to make the difficult and dangerous passage from anarchy to a measure of political community, that is, to a situation in which legal and political processes and institutions settle the argument over power, not the use or threat of mass violence. Thus the "nukephobia" of many religious activists has blinded them to the realities of totalitarian purpose and power as expressed in the Soviet Union, and driven them to a position in which ideological conflict and politics are reduced to a species of psychology ("If we would only understand each other better, there would be peace"). If the harsh facts of nuclear weapons become both the entry point and the controlling reality of our moral analysis, then we will rarely get around to a moral analysis of the disease of international anarchy, and to a careful exploration of what political leadership might do to address that grave problem. This weapons-first style of analysis is why, in my book *Tranquillitas Ordinis,* I described the 1983 Catholic letter as a "weapons pastoral" rather than a "peace pastoral."

Pursuit of the peace of political community in world affairs is a task for just-war theorists and pacifists alike. The contributors spent considerable energy exploring, assessing, and arguing about the various claims of the just-war and pacifist traditions, but did not seem to address the question of what just-war theorists and pacifists might do together for peace. Perhaps, then, a few brief suggestions are in order.

The just-war/pacifist discussion needs to be moved from the level of theoretical debate to the level of practical wisdom. Attempts to blend just-war convictions and pacifist convictions inevitably end up corrupting both (as in the strange hybrid of "nuclear pacifism," wherein a just-war analysis is given the presumed—and questionable—"high moral ground" of "pacifism"). The scholarly debate over the relative weight of just-war and pacifist claims should, and in any event will, continue. But there is another, more practical, discussion to be engaged: the issue of building a measure of rightly ordered political community—peace—in international public life.

There is no reason, for example, why pacifists and just-war theorists cannot work together in defense of those basic human rights (foremost among them, religious liberty), which are so inextricably bound up in the pursuit of peace. Beyond this, pacifists ought to support the democratic revolution in world politics every bit as vigorously as their just-war brethren; democracies do not, historically, war with each other, and democracy is the most successful form of nonviolent conflict resolution known to man. The tragedy of allegedly pacifist organizations supporting, in fact if not in intention, such violent powers as the Nicaraguan Sandinistas comes into its true and depressing focus here.

In sum, then, the great debate over morality and nuclear weapons has to be reconceived as one irreducible dimension of a larger moral argument: the argument over the pursuit of this-worldly peace, which includes within itself the pursuit of liberty and justice. A nuclear weapons debate that is torn from this larger context may well make war more, rather than less, likely, since its public impact will be greatest on those powers whose strategy and policies depend on consent rather than coercion. Peace is not gained by appeasement, even in a nuclear age. Peace is gained through politics.

There is much warranted criticism about the "politicization" of the churches through the nuclear debate. The criticism is most salient when it highlights situations in which contingent political judgments drive the moral analysis, rather than theological convictions and norms. In differing degrees, both the Catholic and Methodist letters suffered from this form of "politicization."

But there is another sense in which the church debate ought to be re-politicized. Peace, in the "engaged" religious community today, is too often conceived as a matter of good will, open communications, and an "understanding" approach to the policies of adversaries. Here, theology has been replaced, not by politics, but by the most oleaginous forms of psychology, indeed of "psychobabble."

The classic Christian tradition, from Augustine through Aquinas, and on to the Reformers, teaches that peace in this world—peace understood not in terms of right relationship with God, or in terms of the eschatological *shalom* kingdom, but as the antonym of war—is a matter of politics, of the right ordering of that distinctive form of human interaction called "political community." To concede the argument over the pursuit of peace to the intellectuals and activists of the therapeutic culture is an abandonment of both theological and political responsibility. It is an abandonment all too frequently encountered in the American religious community, and particularly among its "peace activists." If this volume has done nothing more than to reestablish, as one voice in the debate, the notion that the pursuit of peace, even in a nuclear age, is a matter of the right ordering of human community as an exercise in responsible neighbor-love, then it will have done a needed job in advancing the state of the argument.

Notes

Introduction

1. Roland Bainton, *Christian Attitudes toward War and Peace* (New York: Abingdon Press, 1960), 73.
2. James F. Childress, "Pacifism," in James F. Childress and John Macquarrie, eds., *The Westminster Dictionary of Christian Ethics* (Philadelphia: Westminster Press, 1986), 447.
3. David Hollenbach, *Nuclear Ethics* (New York: Paulist Press, 1983), 43.
4. Michael Novak, *Moral Clarity in a Nuclear Age* (Nashville: Thomas Nelson & Sons, 1983).
5. George Weigel, *Tranquillitas Ordinis: The Present Failure and Future Promise of American Catholic Thought on War and Peace* (New York: Oxford University Press, 1987).

Nuclear Arms in Christian Pacifist Perspective

1. Michael Walzer, *Just and Unjust Wars* (New York: Basic Books/Harper, 1977), 307ff.
2. Ibid., 3ff.
3. There is no one standard list of the criteria to be applied or just how they operate, even in the writings of the most competent interpreters. The most complete summary is the Conspectus in my *Christian Attitudes to War, Peace, and Revolution* (Elkhart, Ind.: Mennonite Coop Bookstore, 1983), 67ff.
4. The most concentrated typological analysis of the varieties of attitudes is that of Geoffrey Nuttall, *Christian Pacifism in History* (Oxford: Basil Blackwell & Mott, 1958; Berkeley: World without War Council, 1971). A broader narrative account is that of Roland

Bainton, *Christian Attitudes to War and Peace* (Nashville: Abingdon Press, 1961).

5. Both of these reasons were represented among the early Christians. Historians debate, in my opinion pointlessly, about the relative weights of the multiple components of the preconstantinian rejection of military service.

6. This was first worked out in the Hussite movement, most solidly expressed by the Czech cobbler theologian Peter Chelcicky, and renewed by Tolstoy. Cf. Peter Brock, *The Political and Social Doctrines of the Unity of Czech Brethren* (The Hague: Mouton, 1957).

7. This view was especially typical of the Swiss Brethren within the left wing of the 16th century Reformation: cf. Ethelbert Stauffer, "Anabaptist Theology of Martyrdom," *Mennonite Quarterly Review* 19 (July 1945): 179ff; Nuttall, *Christian Pacifism in History*, 32ff. James Stayer, *Anabaptists and the* Sword (Lawrence, Kan.: Coronado Press, 1964), 117ff.; and my *Christian Attitudes*, 163–200.

8. This phrase was the first public expression of early Quaker pacifism; Hugh Barbour, *Quakers in Puritan England* (New Haven, Conn.: Yale University Press); and cf. my *Christian Attitudes*, 201ff.

9. This phrase, also from Fox, was to become more meaningful to later Quakers.

10. Such concepts were most classically at home within the monastic and contemplative traditions. They were strong as well in the Pietism from which the Dunkard or Brethren tradition, the third of the historic peace churches, sprang.

11. It was the request of the planners of the Loma Linda conversation that attention should be directed especially to varieties of attitude; the debate is not between alternative tastes or intuitions about war as such nor between differing factual or tactical readings, but rather between clashing systems of moral discourse.

12. That the call to love one's enemy is rooted in the believer's imitation of God as Father is the stated logic of Matt. 5:45 and Luke 6:35.

13. The Barmen Declaration of May 1934 is reprinted in Franklin H. Littell, *The German Phoenix* (Garden City, N.Y.: Doubleday & Co., 1960), 186.

14. National Conference of Catholic Bishops, *The Challenge of Peace* (Washington, D.C.: United States Catholic Conference, 1983).
15. "Statement on Peace and Justice," in David Gill, ed., *Gathered for Life; Official Report, VI Assembly, World Council of Churches* (Geneva and Grand Rapids, Mich.: Eerdmans, 1983), 130ff.; cf. also "Confronting Threats to Peace and Survival," in ibid., 72ff.
16. This position was not really new. It had already been taken by a few of the most qualified theologians in the late 1950s: cf. my *When War Is Unjust* (Minneapolis: Augsburg Publishing House, 1984), 64-67; and my article "Surrender: A Moral Imperative," *Review of Politics* 49 (1986): 560ff. During the last 30 years the continuing growth of the nuclear threat has forced the theologians' principled awareness to trickle up to the bishops.
17. The World Council of Churches statement avoids any formal articulation of its just-war assumptions. The 1986 United Methodists' statement *In Defense of Creation* is no more articulate, since it shifts its concern from killing innocents to endangering our ecology. I gather here a few formal observations of the bishops' letter that were originally solicited from me in several dialogical settings: October 7, 1983, panel on "Ethics and National Security," Indiana Consortium for Security Studies, West Lafayette, Ind.; January 16, 1984, Symposium on the Pastoral Letter, Institute for the Advanced Study of Religion, University of Chicago Divinity School, Chicago, Ill.; April 6, 1984, lecture series "Selected Perspectives on the Bishops' Letter," Catholic University of America, Columbus School of Law, Center for the Study of Law and Religious Traditions, paper published in Charles J. Reid, Jr., ed., *Peace in a Nuclear Age* (Washington, D.C.: Catholic University of America Press, 1986), 273ff. These comments fit within the context of my simpler attempt to envisage how the just-war tradition could become authentically operational in my *When War Is Unjust.* Identifying the limits of *The Challenge of Peace* as a moral treatise does not diminish my great esteem for its originality and courage as a prophetic event.
18. Cf. Edward Laarman, *Nuclear Pacifism: "Just War" Thinking Today* (New York: Peter Lang, 1984).

19. Cf. ibid., 14ff; and my *What Would You Do?* (Scottdale, Pa.: Herald Press, 1983) on the questionable assumptions behind the consequentialist reduction of moral argument to calculation of ends.
20. Cf. Brock, *Pacifism in Europe* (Princeton, N.J.: Princeton University Press, 1972), 442; and *Pacifism in the United States* (Princeton, N.J.: Princeton University Press, 1968), 482–615.
21. The focus on the passivity of nonresistance has been refuted especially by Ronald J. Sider, *Christ and Violence* (Scottdale, Pa.: Herald Press, 1979), 43ff; and by Walter Wink, "The Third Way: Reclaiming Jesus' Nonviolent Alternative," *Sojourners* (December 1986), 28ff.
22. Already in the 1930s Gandhi was being interpreted in the West as a practitioner of nonviolent conflict. Cf. Richard Gregg, *The Power of Non Violence* (New York: J. B. Lippincott, 1934). Now the standard source is Gene Sharp, *The Politics of Non-violent Action* (Boston: Porter Sargent, 1973); cf. also Anders Boserup and Andrew Mack, *War Without Weapons: Non-Violent National Defense* (New York: Schocken Books, 1975).
23. *What Would You Do?* 32ff.
24. Ibid., 21.

Nuclear Deterrence under Strict Moral Conditions

1. National Conference of Catholic Bishops, *The Challenge of Peace: God's Promise and Our Response* (Washington, D.C.: United States Catholic Conference, 1983), hereafter, *CP,* par. 55. For further discussion on the use of Scripture in ethics, see Robert J. Daly, S.J. et al., *Christian Biblical Ethics* (New York: Paulist Press, 1984); William C. Spohn, S.J., *What Are They Saying About Scripture and Ethics?* (New York: Paulist Press, 1984); Allen Verhey, *The Great Reversal: Ethics and the New Testament* (Grand Rapids, Mich.: Eerdmans, 1984); and Thomas Ogletree, *The Use of the Bible in Christian Ethics* (Philadelphia: Fortress Press, 1983).

2. Vatican II, *Pastoral Constitution on the Church in the Modern World,* in *The Sixteen Documents of Vatican II* (Boston: St. Paul Editions, n. d.), par. 80.

3. There is a lively debate among moral theologians today on whether Christian ethics is distinctive from ordinary human morality. See Vincent MacNamara, *Faith and Ethics: Recent Roman Catholicism* (Washington, D.C.: Georgetown University Press, 1985). More emphasis on biblical sources seems to be the direction for a major school in the discipline, although this goes against the predominant tendency to a more "autonomous ethics."

4. For a recent example of an informed and balanced use of these four sources of moral theology, see Lisa Sowle Cahill, *Between the Sexes: Foundations for a Christian Ethics of Sexuality* (Philadelphia: Fortress Press, 1985).

5. See Joseph A. Komonchak, "Kingdom, History, and Church," in *Catholics and Nuclear War,* ed. Philip J. Murnion (New York: Crossroad, 1983), 106–15.

6. See Jay P. Dolan, *The American Catholic Experience: A History from Colonial Times to the Present* (New York: Doubleday & Co., 1985), chaps. 2, 5.

7. For a balanced assessment of what pacifists can learn from just-war advocates and vice-versa see David Hollenbach, S.J., *Nuclear Ethics: A Christian Moral Argument* (New York: Paulist Press, 1983), chap. 2. Hollenbach worked on the staff that prepared the pastoral letter.

8. "In all of this discussion of distinct choices, we are referring to options open to individuals. The council and popes have stated clearly that governments threatened by armed, unjust aggression must defend their people. This includes defense by armed force if necessary as a last resort" (*CP,* 75).

9. Sandra M. Schneiders, "New Testament Reflections on Peace and Nuclear Arms," in *Catholics and Nuclear War,* 91–105.

10. See Richard B. Miller, "Christian Pacifism and Just-War Tenets: How Do They Diverge?" *Theological Studies* 47 (September 1986): 448–72.

11. Francis X. Meehan, "Non-violence and the Bishops' Pastoral: A Case for a Development of Doctrine," in *The Catholic Bishops and Nuclear War,* ed. Judith A. Dwyer, S.S.J. (Washington, D.C.: Georgetown University Press, 1984), 89–107.

12. The trade-off between the cost of weapons and social spending directed toward meeting the basic needs of the poor, i.e., the whole question of justice, is systematically ignored in most discussions of the nuclear arms race. The pastoral letter unequivocally states: "The arms race is one of the greatest curses on the human race; it is to be condemned as a danger, as an act of aggression against the poor, and a folly which does not provide the security it promises" (*CP,* iv).

13. See Gordon Zahn, *War, Conscience and Dissent* (New York: Hawthorn, 1967); James Douglass, *The Non-Violent Cross: A Theology of Revolution and Peace* (New York: Macmillan Co., 1966); and idem, *Lightning East to West: Jesus, Gandhi and the Nuclear Age* (New York: Crossroad, 1983), see also the essays on pacifism in *War or Peace? The Search for New Answers,* ed. Thomas A. Shannon (Maryknoll, N.Y.: Orbis Books, 1980).

14. See James F. Childress, "Just War Criteria," in *War or Peace?,* 42–58; Michael Walzer, *Just and Unjust Wars: A Moral Argument with Historical Illustrations* (New York: Basic Books, 1977).

15. See the collection of essays on this history in *The Journal of Religious Ethics* 12 (Spring 1984); and James T. Johnson, *Can Modern War Be Just?* (New Haven, Conn.: Yale University Press, 1984).

16. "Whereas reasons of state must reject the claim that there are any inherent limits on the means that may be threatened or employed on behalf of the state, *bellum justum* must insist that there are such limits and that they may never be transgressed, whatever the circumstances," Robert W. Tucker, "Morality and Deterrence," in *Nuclear Deterrence: Ethics and Strategy,* ed. Russell Hardin et al. (Chicago: University of Chicago Press, 1985), 55.

17. Hollenbach, *Nuclear Ethics,* 65.

18. See Steven Lee, "The Morality of Nuclear Deterrence: Hostage Holding and Consequences," in *Nuclear Deterrence: Ethics and Strategy,* eds. Russell Hardin, John J. Mearsheimer, Gerald Dworkin,

and Robert E. Goodin (Chicago: University of Chicago Press, 1985), 173–90.

19. "Although we acknowledge the need for deterrent, not all forms of deterrence are morally acceptable. There are moral limits to deterrence policy as well as to policy regarding use" (*CP*, 178).

20. Moral criticism of present deterrence postures does not necessarily connote an absolute moral prohibition of deterrence in any form, argues John Langan, S.J., "The American Hierarchy and Nuclear Weapons," *Theological Studies* 43 (September 1982): 447–67.

21. For a perceptive analysis of this statement and its role in the pastoral letter, see Bruce M. Russett, "The Doctrine of Deterrence," in *Catholics and Nuclear War,* 149–67. Russett was a consultant to the bishops' committee that composed the letter.

22. J. Bryan Hehir, "Moral Issues in Deterrence Policy," in Douglas MacLean, *The Security Gamble: Deterrence Dilemma in the Nuclear Age* (Totowa, N.J.: Rowman & Allenheld, 1984), 60. Hehir was the principal staff writer for the various drafts of the pastoral letter.

23. "We are told that some weapons are designed for purely 'counterforce' use against military forces and targets. The moral issue, however, is not resolved by the design of weapons or the planned intention for use; there are also consequences which must be assessed. It would be a perverted political policy or moral casuistry which tried to justify using a weapon which 'indirectly' or 'unintentionally' killed a million innocent people because they happened to live near a 'militarily significant target' " (*CP*, 193).

24. See *Nuclear Ethics,* 37–46.

25. For an excellent review of these reactions see James W. McGray, "Nuclear Deterrence: Is the War-and-Peace Pastoral Inconsistent?" *Theological Studies* 46 (December 1983): 700–10; see also Richard A. McCormick, S.J., "Notes on Moral Theology: 1983," *Theological Studies* 45 (March 1984): 80–138; and David Hollenbach, S.J., "Notes on Moral Theology: 1985," *Theological Studies* 47 (March 1986): 117–33.

26. See Matthew 5–7; Luke 6, Romans 12–15, Galatians 5.

27. Robert McKim, "An Examination of a Moral Argument Against Nuclear Deterrence," *Journal of Religious Ethics* 13 (Fall 1985): 287.

Notes

28. David Hoekema, "Morality, Just War, and Nuclear Weapons: An Analysis of 'The Challenge of Peace,' " *Soundings* 67 (1984): 365.
29. Although both positions invoke religious warrants to support their judgment of human life as inviolable, I want to treat them as philosophical deontologists here. For a persuasive account of the irrelevance of consequences for Christians engaged in social resistance, see John Howard Yoder, *The Politics of Jesus* (Grand Rapids, Mich.: Eerdmans, 1972), 233–250.
30. Russell Shaw, "The Bishops and Deterrence: What Next?" *America,* September 7, 1985, 101–103.
31. For a pacifist critique of the letter, see Gordon C. Zahn, "Pacifism and the Just War," in *Catholics and Nuclear War,* 119–31.
32. J. Bryan Hehir argues that this concern for both values reflects the approach of the "church" type of organization rather than the "sect" type of organization, borrowing the now-classic models of Ernest Troeltsch. See "Church-Type Reinvigorated: The Bishops' Letter," in *Peace, Politics and the People of God,* ed. Paul Peachey (Philadelphia: Fortress Press, 1986), 47–67.
33. I do not mean to imply that all, or even most, pacifists are unconcerned about the consequences of a policy of unilateral disarmament. However, their prophetic witness concentrates more on the moral horror of our present situation than on practical alternatives. I also realize that in a world with such a history of violence our imaginations may be stunted by skepticism about the viability of nonviolent alternatives.
34. See Richard M. Gula, S.S., *What Are They Saying About Moral Norms?* (New York: Paulist Press, 1982); the major essays on the subject over the last 20 years are collected in *Readings in Moral Theology No. 1: Moral Norms and Catholic Tradition,* ed. Charles E. Curran and Richard A. McCormick, S.J. (New York: Paulist Press, 1979); Lisa Sowle Cahill "Teleology, Utilitarianism, and Christian Ethics," *Theological Studies* 42 (December 1981): 601–29.
35. Robert W. Tucker of Johns Hopkins School of Advanced International Studies notes that the bishops separated the question of warfare from deterrence: "This near absolute condemnation of

nuclear war cannot but have a bearing on the moral assessment of deterrence. If nuclear weapons are by their very nature illegitimate because their use cannot be controlled or their effects limited, must not deterrence structures that rest on the threat to use nuclear weapons also be in principle illegitimate? So it would seem. But the rejection of nuclear war is one thing and the rejection of deterrence quite another. What the bishops have done is to tie a moral theory to a particular view of deterrence. The principles governing the just conduct of war have been linked to a strategic doctrine [i.e., a purely war-deterring and not a war-fighting strategy, sufficiency not superiority] . . . they have also endowed their chosen view with minimal moral acceptability while judging as morally unacceptable the alternative view" Tucker, *Nuclear Deterrence,* 67.

36. McGray, "Nuclear Deterrence: Is the War-and-Peace Pastoral Inconsistent?" 700–10.

37. Ibid., 707.

38. Ibid., 708.

39. Ibid., 709. Obviously, his rationale is a form of consequentialist argumentation, but not a strictly utilitarian one since it considers the moral quality of acts themselves.

40. Robert McKim employs another form of consequentialist reasoning to argue that "conditional intentions are wrong if they contribute to the production of wrong actions, irrespective of what view we take of what *makes* actions right or wrong" (McKim, "An Examination," 293). Nuclear deterrence is prima facie wrong since it leads us closer to nuclear disaster. It is a case of threatening to do what is known to be wrong to do with discernible intentions to carry out that threat. "Deterrence seems to involve something wrong being permitted for the sake of a greater good. This situation is morally unacceptable if there is a way to attain the good without involving the evil" (ibid., 294). He maintains that this situation makes seeking a way out of our present standoff a moral imperative.

41. "In the past few years this confidence and sense of stability [in MAD] have been shattered. Both sides began to fear that their

capacity for retaliatory strikes might be destroyed by more precise and more powerful weapons in 'first strike' by the other side.

". . . the rather recent realization that nuclear war would not only kill many scores or hundreds of millions of contemporaries and increase the degree of destruction of the contemporary institutions of civilization that we have known in previous wars, but it would also seriously damage the earthly and atmospheric environment of most or all of humanity, the support systems of this and even future generations. This is the essential dividing line between past wars and nuclear wars," John C. Bennett, "Nuclear Deterrence Is Itself Vulnerable," *Christianity and Crisis,* August 13, 1984, 296–301.

Bennett himself supported the development of the hydrogen bomb as a deterrent to the Soviet threat in Western Europe in a study commissioned by the Federal Council of Churches in 1950. They did not oppose first use of nuclear weapons under all circumstances.

42. Michael MccGwire, "Dilemmas and Delusions of Deterrence," *World Policy Journal* 1 (1984).

The Just-War Legacy in the Nuclear Age

1. George Weigel, *Tranquillitas Ordinis: The Present Failure and Future Promise of American Catholic Thought on War and Peace* (New York: Oxford University Press, 1987).
2. See ibid.
3. See Richard Grenier, "The Gandhi Nobody Knows," *Commentary* 75 (March 1983): 66–67.
4. Ibid.
5. Albert Wohlstetter, "Bishops, Statesmen, and Other Strategists on the Bombing of Innocents," *Commentary* 75 (June 1983), 18.
6. Weigel, *Tranquillitas Ordinis,* 391-92.

Comment by John C. Bennett

1. Morgenthau Memorial Lecture, 1988, published by the Carnegie Council on Ethics and International Affairs, New York..
2. Mikhail S. Gorbachev, *Perestroika* (New York: Harper & Row, 1987).
3. Ibid., 145.
4. Ibid., 145, 157.
5. *Russia* (New York: Atheneum, 1976), 406.
6. "Swollen Society, Spent Society: Stalin's Legacy to Brezhnev's Russia," *Foreign Affairs* (Winter 1981–82), 431–32.

Suggested Readings

Historical Surveys

ROLAND BAINTON, *Christian Attitudes toward War and Peace: A Historical Survey and Critical Re-Evaluation* (New York: Abingdon Press, 1960).

This modern classic provides a lucid, orderly, and well-documented guide to the major figures and perennial issues in Christian thinking on war. Bainton's analysis yields the memorable categories of pacifism, just-war theories, and the crusade.

ALBERT MARRIN, ed., *War and the Christian Conscience: From Augustine to Martin Luther King, Jr.* (Chicago: Henry Regnery, 1971).

This anthology contains helpful selections from Tertullian, Origen, Augustine, St. Thomas, Martin Luther, Thomas Müntzer, George Fox, Leo Tolstoy, Paul Ramsey, and many others. The anthology is organized under four headings: (1) early Christianity and the problem of war, (2) the Christian as warrior, (3) the pacifist tradition, and (4) the bomb and after.

Pacifism

JOHN HOWARD YODER, *The Original Revolution* (Scottdale, Pa.: Herald Press, 1972).

Yoder, perhaps the leading Christian pacifist thinker, demonstrates the wide-ranging scope of his commitment in these essays on Christian pacifism.

GUY F. HERSHBERGER, *War, Peace, and Nonresistance,* 3d ed. (Scottdale, Pa.: Herald Press, 1969).

The author, from within the historic peace church tradition, has written a notable, comprehensive work on Christian pacifism in faith and history.

DONALD B. KRAYBILL, *Facing Nuclear War: A Plea for Christian Witness* (Scottdale, Pa.: Herald Press, 1982).

Christian pacifist Kraybill's popularly written appeal for Christian action combines Christian and political arguments in discussing "the chief moral issue of our time." His book, written from an evangelical perspective, is composed for those who have not yet thought extensively about how their faith relates to the nuclear era, and is excellent for lay discussion groups.

JENNY TEICHMAN, *Pacifism and the Just War: A Study in Applied Pacifism* (Worcester, Eng.: Basil Blackwell, 1986).

This philosophical treatment of pacifism and just-war thinking sees them as complementary sets of doctrines. Teichman argues that a sane appropriation of either tradition views war as intrinsically evil, and could lead to the forced option of war as the lesser of two intrinsically evil options. Pacifism, Teichman concludes, has the advantage of being more serious about abolishing war.

Just-War Theory

PAUL RAMSEY, *The Just War: Force and Political Responsibility* (New York: Charles Scribner's Sons, 1968).

Political life cannot endure without use of force, and neither can a nation win at bargaining that for which it is not willing to fight. A just war, however, can never deliberately kill innocent people. Thus Ramsey argues that for the terms *just war* and *unjust war* we substitute *counterforce* and *counter-people* warfare. Whereas the killing of non-combatants cannot be justified, counter-force warfare can be.

JOHN HOWARD YODER, *When War Is Unjust: Being Honest in Just-War Thinking* (Minneapolis: Augsburg Publishing House, 1984).

The author asks hard questions of the just-war tradition in terms of its own tenets and demonstrates considerable pragmatic commonality between just-war theory and Christian pacifism.

DAVID HOLLENBACH, S.J., *Nuclear Ethics: A Christian Moral Argument* (New York: Paulist Press, 1983).

Written by a thinker who helped formulate the U.S. Catholic bishops' pastoral letter, this book is concise, candid, and penetrating in its treatment of issues; the indebtedness of just-war thinking; and the final but necessary inconsistency in continued use of nuclear deterrence.

MICHAEL WALZER, *Just and Unjust Wars: A Moral Argument with Historical Illustrations* (New York: Basic Books, 1977).

A philosophical and historical analysis of just-war thinking in the nuclear age, this book concludes that finally no moral theory can do justice to the competing claims of individual human rights and collective survival.

Just Nuclear Defense

GEORGE WEIGEL, *Tranquillitas Ordinis: The Present Failure and Future Promise of American Catholic Thought on War and Peace* (New York: Oxford University Press, 1987).

The author describes this volume as a "lover's quarrel with my church." Weigel believes that the Roman Catholic Church in the

U.S. in the last few years has largely abandoned its distinctive understanding of "peace" as "dynamic and rightly ordered political community" *(tranquillities ordinis)*. Thus this project of reclamation of past insights and development of a "politics of peace and freedom."

MICHAEL NOVAK, *Moral Clarity in a Nuclear Age* (Nashville: Thomas Nelson & Sons, 1983).

This lucid and provocative Catholic lay theologian here presents the politically and religiously conservative answer to the U.S. Catholic bishops' pastoral on peace. Three other essays are also included: one, a European-oriented perspective on the nuclear arms challenge; another on the changes made in the bishops' pastoral letter in late 1982 and early 1983; and a final chapter on just—and unjust—negotiations.

JAMES TURNER JOHNSON, *Can Modern War Be Just?* (New Haven, Conn.: Yale University Press, 1984).

A foremost student of just-war theory applies himself to the contemporary debate. He argues for the moral duty to develop warfare strategies that can justifiably be employed to counter threats when use of force is the only means available. Although the limits of just-war thinking normally apply, in a worst-case scenario Turner allows that one may in specific cases temporarily go beyond the limits and even kill non-combatants in doing what must be done to further one's own just cause when the enemy's injustice is plain.

PAUL SEABURY AND ANGELO CODEVILLA, *War: Ends and Means* (New York: Basic Books, 1989).

The authors explore various aspects of war: causes, methods, results, and justifications. The notion that peace is always to be preferred over war is seen as illusory and naive.

Ecclesiastical Documents

PHILIP J. MURNION, ed., *Catholics and Nuclear War: A Commentary on "The Challenge of Peace," the U.S. Catholic Bishops' Pastoral Letter on War and Peace* (New York: Crossroad, 1983).
In addition to containing the full text of the bishops' pastoral letter, this volume contains essays on various aspects of the pastoral by such thinkers as David Hollenbach, Charles Curran, J. Bryan Hehir, Lester C. Thurow, and Richard A. McCormick.

JAMES V. SCHALL, S.J., ed., *Out of Justice, Peace* (Joint Pastoral Letter of the West German Bishops, 1983); and *Winning the Peace* (Joint Pastoral Letter of the French Bishops, 1983) (San Francisco: Ignatius Press, 1984).
The statements issued by two groups of European national Catholic bishops are noted for their politically more conservative stance when compared with the U.S. bishops' pastoral.

The United Methodist Council of Bishops, *In Defense of Creation: The Nuclear Crisis and a Just Peace* (Nashville: Graded Press, 1986).
The result of a two-year study, this document represents the most complete statement on the nuclear crisis ever issued by the Council of Bishops.